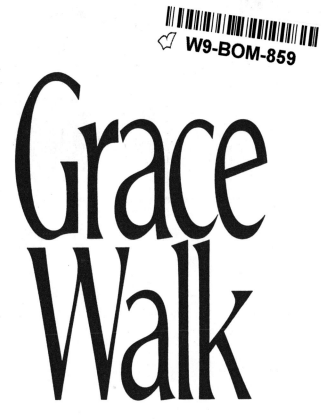

Grace Walk

Steve McVey

Harvest House Publishers
Eugene, Oregon 97402

GRACE WALK

Copyright © 1995 by Harvest House Publishers
Eugene, Oregon 97402

Library of Congress Cataloging-in-Publication Data

McVey, Steve, 1954–
    Grace walk / Steve McVey.
        p.   cm.
    ISBN 1-56507-3215
    1. Christian life.   2. McVey, Steve, 1954–   . I. Title
BV4501.2.M4367   1995
248.4—dc20   94-47485
                                                                           CIP

Printed in the United States of America.

96 97 98 99 00 — 10 9 8 7 6 5 4 3 2

To Melanie,
my most precious grace gift
in this world.

Acknowledgments

Numerous people have influenced the publishing of this book. It is a pleasure to acknowledge a few of them. I am especially grateful to Bill Gillham, who first read the manuscript and called me early one morning with enthusiastic affirmation. He initiated the process that would ultimately lead to this publication. Through their warm encouragement, Bob Hawkins, Jr. and Eileen Mason of Harvest House caused me to catch the vision for the work necessary to bring this book to fruition. The most helpful input in revising the book came from Bob Welch. As I followed each of his editorial suggestions, I watched the book open from bud to full bloom. I appreciate Steve Miller's attentive oversight to the publication process.

This book was formed in my heart before it was typed on paper. God used many friends to fan the fire of grace in me, but I am especially grateful to a group of intimate friends I met with each week. The love and affirmation of this "Grace Group" instilled faith within me to trust God to bring to pass all that He had placed in my heart. Special thanks to Bob and Sheree Lykens, Keith and Vernois Wilson, Ray and Jill Wtulich, Tony and Sherry Gordon, Danny and Sue Feagin, Ron and Wylene Buchannan, Jack and Shelly Nelson, and Cheryl Buchannan. The weekly fellowship with you dear friends ministered to me so much.

God has used many other people in molding my faith. I especially appreciate my many friends in Talladega, Alabama whose love and encouragement was such a blessing. You folks will always hold a special place in my heart.

I also want to thank my family. My wife, Melanie, is a treasure who has always inspired and encouraged me. That fact was especially true as the book progressed. I appreciate the willingness of my children—Andrew, Amy, David, and Amber—to give up time with their dad to allow him opportunity to write. No kids have been more loved.

Finally, I thank God for His gracious leading in writing this book. The Holy Spirit gave me the desire to write my testimony, incorporating the truths of our identity in Christ into it. When I began to write, I had no thoughts of it being published. Our loving Father initiated it and completed it. I give Him the glory for whatever good may come from this book.

CONTENTS

FOREWORD

Grace Walk is not a *good* book. Good books are most often read because they're the current rage. Then they're discussed for a bit at the office the next day, set on the shelf, and forgotten. This is a *great* book, one you'll go back to again and again! Steve McVey has mined some diamonds from what the Bible calls the "mystery" of the gospel, which is our identity in Christ. He does an excellent job of explaining how believers can make these truths their own reality.

In order to write this book, Steve had to discover that some truths are better learned on your back than on your feet. After many years of "successful" pastoring, God let Steve's productive techniques become about as effective as screen doors on a submarine. In so doing, God taught him a truth which many of us miss: the key to experiencing supernatural, liberating strength is *personal weakness*. That's right, personal weakness. God's power "shows up best in weak people" (2 Corinthians 12:9, TLB). Steve uses his biblical understanding and communication skills to share with us what Paul discovered: The weaker you are, the more God's strength can "show up" in you.

Most of us begin by believing that God wants *strong* folks to help Him accomplish His work; the truth is that the world is designed to *wear down* those who trust in their own strength. Through this wearing-down process, God teaches us to place our confidence in Christ, not in our own flesh. As Steve points out so skillfully, it's not God's plan that we go through our entire earth walk living a defeated Christian life: in fact, it's abnormal for us to do so. God never intended for us to live a supernatural life. Jesus Christ, the supernatural Son of God, is the only One who ever *has* and who still *does* live supernaturally—through Christians who let Him do so. Amazing as it may seem, Christ is even more than Savior and Lord; He is our very *Life* (Colossians 3:1-4). Steve does an excellent job of using scriptural documentation to show us that God's plan is for you and the "Spirit of Christ" to cohabit our earthsuit and become dear, intimate friends as together we experience victory over the world, the flesh, and the devil.

I heartily recommend *Grace Walk* to every Christian desiring an intimate walk with Jesus Christ. You're in for an exciting read.

Bill Gillham
Fort Worth, Texas

CHAPTER 1

MISERABLE MEDIOCRITY

t was at 1:00 A.M. on October 6, 1990, that I lay on my face in my office, crying. The previous year had brought me to a place of absolute brokenness. I had prayed for God to make me stronger, but He had a different plan. He was making me weaker. So there I lay, broken and hopeless. In seventeen hours I would have to stand in my pulpit on Sunday evening and deliver a "State of the Church Address"? Either I could build a straw man of success or I could tell the truth. I didn't have the strength to pretend or the courage to be honest, so I prayed and cried. When I finished, I prayed and cried some more.

It didn't make sense. Had God brought me to this church only to set me up for failure? Couldn't He see that I was doing everything I knew how for Him? I couldn't imagine what more He expected from me than my best. And I *had* done my best. *God, what more do You want from me?* Silence. At this moment He seemed light-years away. The weight of failure was suffocating, and not just my failure as a pastor. I felt like a failure as a Christian. If dedicating my whole adult life to God to do His work wasn't enough, what more did He want?

I had left a church in Alabama where I felt very successful, where people loved and affirmed me. Our church was recognized for its numerical growth, and we led the denomination in baptisms in our county. I received recognition from the Jaycees for being an "outstanding young religious leader." I served on various denominational committees and held office in our ministers' conference. For five years, I believed I was a successful pastor.

Then one Saturday afternoon the telephone rang. "Would you be willing to allow our pastor search committee to attend your church and hear you preach? Then we would like to have lunch with you and your family after the service." I had declined this kind of invitation numerous times in the past few years. Yet I sensed during the first conversation with the chairman of this pastor search committee that I should let these folks come.

After many weeks of contact with each other, I decided that God was indeed bringing us together. A few months later, Melanie, our four kids, and I found ourselves following a moving van across Interstate 20 toward Atlanta. Our new church had been declining in attendance for several years, but every congregation I had served had consistently grown, and I was confident that this one would too. I unpacked my books, my sermons, and my church growth programs, anxious to get started. We had moved from a small town to the big city, and there were lots of people just waiting to be reached!

I pulled out my box of sugar-stick sermons and previously proven programs and went to work for God.

But nothing happened. This was a new experience and I was puzzled. I reassessed the situation, prayed harder for God's help, took a deep breath, and launched my second wave of church growth plans. We had sanctified pep rallies with our Sunday school teachers, strategy sessions with church leaders, and long-range planning discussions with our newly formed Dream Team. But as the months passed, the dream began to look more like a nightmare. As I approached the end of my first year as pastor, I had told the people that I would share a "State of the Church" address on my first anniversary. Now, as I examined the measurable progress during the past year, I knew that our church was in a sorry state. For the first time in my seventeen years of ministry, a church I served had declined in attendance during my first year. I was appalled!

When one feels like a failure, especially in a culture that places so much importance on success, there is a dull pain that can't fully be described. In the movie *City Slickers*, Mitch, the character played by Billy Crystal, is talking to a friend at work on his thirty-ninth birthday. He asks, "Do you ever reach a point in your life when you say, 'This is the best I'll ever look, the best I'll ever feel, the best I'm ever gonna do, and it ain't that great'?"

American culture demands that we be successful. People often measure our significance by what we have accomplished. From the time our parents applauded our first steps, we have been conditioned to seek approval and acceptance from others by what we do. That fact puts unbelievable pressure on us to succeed.

This demand for success doesn't stop outside the doors of the church. Many Christians are struggling to make their lives count for Christ, only to discover that the Christian life isn't working out like it's supposed to. They are sincere about their commitment to Christ and have given it their best effort. Yet, they are frustrated because they can't live up to what they think a Christian ought to be. They've concluded that their spiritual life is about as good as it's ever gonna get, and it ain't that great.

There Must Be More Than This!

Bible teacher Charles Trumbull described his spiritual frustrations this way:

> There were great fluctuations in my spiritual life, in my conscious closeness of fellowship with God. Sometimes I would be on the heights spiritually; sometimes I would be in the depths. A strong, arousing convention, a stirring, searching address from some consecrated, victorious Christian leader of men; a searching Spirit-filled book; or the obligation to do a difficult piece of Christian service myself, with the preparation in prayer that it involved, would lift me up; and I would stay up for a while and God would seem very close and my spiritual life deep. But it wouldn't last. Sometimes by some single failure before temptation, sometimes by a gradual downhill process, my best experiences would be lost, and I would find myself back on the lower levels. And a lower level is a perilous place for a Christian to be, as the devil showed me over and over again.[1]

Sound familiar? It may describe the way you feel right now. I became a Christian at the age of eight, and Trumbull's description of his Christian experience pretty much parallels mine for the next twenty-nine years after I trusted Christ. I don't think I've been alone in this. Many who have professed Christ as Savior have secretly wondered, "Is *this* all there is to it? Surely the Christian life is meant to be more!" They *know* that they are supposed to be experiencing the abundant life Jesus promised, yet they find themselves in a life of mediocrity. These Christians want a victorious Christian life, but they don't know how to find it.

Matt was a young man who struggled with an addiction to illegal drugs and alcohol. I had given him all the pat answers about reading the Bible more and praying harder. But here he was again sitting in my office, wanting my help. "It's not that I don't want to live for God," he said. "I pray for Him to help me and I really mean it, but things just never seem to change." I knew he meant it. His sincerity was obvious. That's what frustrated me. I had told him the same answers over and over again, but they weren't working for him.

In one way, Matt and I weren't all that different. No, I wasn't addicted to drugs or alcohol, my sins were far more respectable than that. But, in spite of all my efforts to be free, I could still point to areas of my life where I felt enslaved. Until God revealed the key to enjoying victory in the Christian life, I tried a lot of things that didn't work. And Matt and I weren't alone in this frustration. Maybe you can relate to some of our efforts to find the fulfillment you have hungered for.

If at First You Don't Succeed . . .

We live in a culture that commends effort. From

childhood we have been told, "Don't give up. Don't be a quitter. Keep trying until you accomplish your goal." You've seen the Avis ad, "We try harder!" In the natural world, trying harder is commendable and often effective. But God's ways aren't our ways. Sometimes they seem to be opposite from ours. In the spiritual world, trying harder is detrimental. That's right. Trying harder will defeat you every time.

No Christian has a problem with the previous paragraph as it relates to salvation. If an unsaved person were to suggest to you that he was trying hard to become a Christian, what would you tell him? You would probably make it clear that he could not be saved by *trying*, but by *trusting*. You would tell him that there is absolutely nothing he could do to gain salvation. It has all already been done. Salvation is a gift to be received, not a reward to be earned. A person who tries even a little bit to gain salvation by works cannot become a Christian. As Paul said about salvation, "If by grace, then it is no longer of works; otherwise grace is no longer grace. But if it is of works, it is no longer grace; otherwise work is no longer work" (Romans 11:6). In other words, it has to be either grace or works. We are saved by grace, and trying hard has absolutely nothing to do with it.

But many Christians who understand that trying is detrimental to becoming a Christian somehow think that it is essential to living in victory after salvation. The truth is that victory is not a reward but a gift. A person does not experience victory in the Christian life by trying hard to live for God. It just won't work! I know because that's what I did. Have you *tried* to live for God? Did your efforts cause you to experience real victory? I rest my case . . . temporarily.

I lived many years of my Christian life trapped in what I call the motivation-condemnation-rededication cycle. From the earliest years of my Christian life, I had a mental picture of what I thought I should be. In this picture there was always a wide gap between where I ought to be and where I was. Sometimes when I was especially motivated, I would feel that the gap had narrowed a bit. When I was winning people to Christ or spending a lot of time praying and studying the Bible, I felt that I might actually one day be able to bridge the gap and be a victorious Christian.

But inevitably, my motivation level would diminish and my fury and fire would die down. That decline always led to a sense of condemnation. Even when I had done nothing wrong, I would feel guilty for not doing all the things that I believed I should be doing. The devil had a field day with me during this phase. Sometimes I would become spiritually indifferent. Other times I would wonder if I would ever be consistent in my Christian life. I would wallow in my misery until I couldn't stand it anymore; then I would finally rededicate myself to God, confessing my spiritual slothfulness. With genuine contempt for my inconsistency, I would ask God to help me be more consistent. I would promise to read my Bible more, pray more, win more souls, whatever I thought it took to get back on course. I resolved to try harder than ever to live for God. Yet no matter how hard I tried, I never experienced real peace about my Christian life. If I read five chapters of the Bible, I felt that I should have read ten. If I led one person to Christ, I thought it should have been two. My wife, Melanie, used to tell me, "You'll never be satisfied." I was a classic Type A personality trying hard to do something for God. It was a miserable ride on a spiritual roller coaster!

Many other people have acknowledged a similar experience. They live in this vicious cycle, moving from motivation to condemnation to rededication. If this describes your spiritual life, after a while this constant spinning around and around will make you sick. But I want to give you hope. There *is* a way to get off this ride! I know because I got off this nauseating roller coaster, and I have found the Christian life to be much more wonderful since then.

You Know the Rules!

An important cornerstone of a civilized society is law. Without laws to govern the behavior of its citizens, a nation would exist in anarchy. Webster's defines law as, "a rule or order that it is advisable or obligatory to observe."[2] We have all been taught that if we don't obey the rules, we will be punished. Whether it is a child sneaking cookies before dinner or an adult driving 70 in a 55-mph zone, if we get caught breaking the rules, we pay the price. Because we are taught from the cradle to the coffin that we must obey the law, it is very natural to transfer this system into the Christian life.

The law of God is good because it accomplishes an important function. But many Christians have misunderstood the purpose of the law. The law was given so that people might see their own absolute inadequacy to live in a way that glorifies God. In the Old Testament the law revealed to Israel God's righteous standard. The story of the Hebrew people chronicles their repeated failure to live up to God's laws. Because God is omniscient, He knew before He gave the law that they wouldn't keep it.

Through the law God revealed that righteousness

cannot come from external regulations. Every person understands this at the time of salvation, but many seem to believe that the rules change *after* they are saved. Some who are quick to point out that keeping religious rules won't cause anybody to become a Christian believe that keeping certain rules will help them grow in the Christian life. These folks spend great amounts of time tying to improve their spiritual performance.

After the service one Sunday morning, Vicki came to me with tears in her eyes. "Steve, can I talk to you a minute?" We walked to the office area and sat down. Nervously fidgeting with a crumpled Kleenex, she began to cry. "I don't know what I'm supposed to do. I have rededicated myself to God over and over again. I'm reading my Bible, although I don't seem to get much out of it these days. I set my clock to get up early and spend time in prayer. I even agreed to work in the children's church so that I could serve the Lord there. But I still feel empty. I've asked God if I'm unhappy because of some sin in my life, but I can't think of anything. Why don't I have the joy that Christians are supposed to experience?"

Vicki is typical of many Christians. Instead of experiencing joy in Christ, she was trying to find fulfillment through her Christian lifestyle. Her lack of contentment caused her to believe that God must not be pleased with her.

I can certainly relate to her experience. For many years I thought that God accepted me more when I served Him as I thought He wanted me to do. I knew that He always loved me, but felt that He probably didn't really like me at times. I pictured God sitting in heaven keeping His patience like a parent whose anger is about to explode if the child's conduct doesn't improve soon. When I was in a motivation phase, I would do as much as possible to gain His approval. One time a friend and I agreed that we wouldn't eat until we led someone to Christ. We started out visiting hardened "prospects" and gradually worked our way down as we became increasingly hungry. Finally, we got a kid bicycling in the park to pray the sinner's prayer; then we made a beeline to McDonald's!

Sometimes I would fast and pray for hours. Once I spent three days in my office without coming out. At the end of my "time with God," I was starving and dirty, but didn't feel any closer to God! Don't miss my point. I am not suggesting that it is wrong to witness to unsaved people, or to fast and pray. I am saying that it was ridiculous to have thought it was somehow possible to cause God to accept me more than He already did.

I can't tell you how many times I have heard people lament a lack of fulfillment in their Christian life and then conclude that the answer was to get back in church, witness more, start tithing, or pray more. Take it from one who did all those things and still felt unfulfilled—polishing your performance is not the answer! Some of the most miserable people in the world are drowning in a sea of religious activity. The sad thing is that they are absolutely sincere. Can you relate to this? If you can, stay tuned, because I've got some good news for you!

Why Can't I Be Successful?

Some people think that ministers have it all together, but I'll let you in on a secret. Sometimes I don't have it all together. In fact, at times I've felt that it was all falling apart! Preachers are just like other people in many ways. A friend of our son David came home with us after church one Sunday afternoon. That evening he went home and told his mother, "They're just like us!" It's good he figured that out early in life. Pastors don't speak King James English. We sometimes yell at our kids and argue with our wives and worry about our bills. We can even act like idiots, laughing at silly things. Some of us are Trekkies. We know about Indiana Jones and Rambo. We might even offer an opinion about David Letterman moving from NBC to CBS.

Got the picture? I'm just a regular guy like you.

There is something else pastors have in common with other Christians. We all have had the desire to be successful in our spiritual life. The popular belief is that success comes by commitment and hard work. That's true in the business world. A person dedicated to accomplishing something in business has every reason to be optimistic about his chances in our free enterprise system. But it doesn't work that way in the spiritual life.

The criterion for measuring success in the world is production. The person who produces impressive results in business is considered successful. Successful people have learned how to accomplish the desired results. But here is where we get into trouble in the Christian life. Christianity isn't built around performance, but is centered on the person of Jesus Christ.

When we transfer a worldly approach to success to the Christian life, we are in for disappointment. And, unfortunately, this understanding of spiritual success has infiltrated the modern church. When Paul met the brethren, he greeted them with the words "grace" and "peace." Today pastors often greet each other with words like "How many are you running now? What's your budget? How many baptisms did you have last year?" I am embarrassed to admit how often I have asked those questions in the past. My concept of success in the church was tied to production and performance. I had the same understanding about my personal life. I thought that to be a successful Christian, I must read the Bible enough, pray enough, do enough evangelistic outreach—more production and performance. My whole life was wrapped up in rules and routine. Have you experienced this in your life? It was a thrilling day when I finally came to understand that Christianity is not rules and routine, but a relationship! God never intended for our focus to be on performing and producing. He desires that our focus be on the person of Jesus Christ!

So many Christians today measure the success of their spiritual lives by whether they live up to religious rules. They focus on their performance. They try to live up to the standard they have set for themselves, but they can never do enough. No wonder they feel defeated!

When Christians try to live by rules, the outcome will be the same as it has always been. They will discover that they just can't measure up, regardless of how hard they try. The law is intended to make people realize, "I just can't do it. I've tried and tried, but I just can't live a successful Christian life." If that's how you feel, then you might be closer than you know to enjoying success. Your sense of failure may be the catalyst God wants to use to bring you to a new understanding of the meaning of the Christian life.

For a long time I thought that to experience success

in my Christian life, I had to work harder. But I discovered that the key to enjoying success is not strenuous work, but spiritual rest. This is a paradox in Scripture—we must rest while we work! Many Christians feel like spiritual failures. Satan knows that as long as he can keep them feeling and thinking like defeated failures, they will behave that way.

There is a way to enjoy a successful Christian life every day! There is a quality of Christian living that I didn't know existed until twenty-nine years after I was saved. I don't blame you if you don't believe it yet. Just don't close your mind to the possibility that there might be more to the Christian life than you are experiencing right now.

All those years when I struggled to do something for God, I was sincere. And God graciously gave me some wonderful times in my Christian life and ministry. But then He began a work in my life greater than anything I had ever known. But it wasn't a happy process. In fact, God's work in my life had brought me to the place where I lay on the floor wondering whether or not I would continue in the ministry. My feelings were beyond disappointment or even discouragement. I felt despair. *God, if this is all that ministry will ever be, I want out. I just want to quit.* I think God must have smiled, because that's exactly what He had been waiting to hear. Now what He would do in my life would make the former days look mediocre at best.

CHAPTER 2

DARKNESS BEFORE DAWN

or a couple of agonizing hours I lay on the floor behind my desk. It was almost 2 A.M. and I had no tears left. The pressure of anxiety which had built up over the previous year had been released in this unexpected burst of emotion. Now I just felt tired and empty. In the stillness of the early morning hour, my thoughts turned to a piece of paper that someone had given me a few weeks earlier. I reached up to my computer desk, took the sheet, and began to read it. It was a quotation about absolute surrender to God. On one side was a list of things to commit to God. On the other side was a list of rights to give up—things like the right to success, the right to acceptance, the right to pleasant circumstances, the right to results. I took that paper and began to pray my way down the list. *Lord, I'm tired of struggling for victory in my own life and I am tired of striving for success in my ministry.* As I continued to pray, I chose to lay aside everything that had brought me a sense of worth: my efforts to have a growing church, my hunger for

25

affirmation in ministry, my education, and my experience. As I came to the bottom of the list, I read this paragraph:

> I give God permission to do anything He wishes to me, with me, in me, or through me that would glorify Him. I once claimed these rights as mine, but now they belong to God and are under His control. He can do with them anything He pleases.

Although I didn't understand the full implications of absolute surrender, I signed my name below that paragraph. I sensed that this night was a turning point in my life and ministry. Before I finally went home to sleep, I wrote these words in my spiritual journal:

> On this morning between midnight and 2:00 A.M., God's Holy Spirit has done a redemptive work in my heart by consuming me with Himself. Details are too personal and sacred to even write, but it is a work of His grace in me like nothing I have ever known in over eighteen years. May this be my "Ebenezer" to mark the moment of a life-altering encounter with Him. "Then Samuel took a stone, and set it up between Mizpeh and Shen, and called its name Ebenezer, saying, "Thus far the Lord has helped us" (1 Samuel 7:12).

When I left my office that morning, I didn't want a new program or plan. I wanted only one thing—Him.

I stood up in church the next night and shared with the congregation how I had met with God the previous night. I told them that I felt led to suspend all programs and activity and simply begin to seek God. I shared with them that the Lord had impressed these words on my mind: "That I may know Him and the power of His resurrection, and the fellowship of His sufferings, being conformed to His death" (Philippians 3:10). I told our church family that our need was not for a new and improved approach to ministry, but rather for a more intimate knowledge of God Himself.

God met with us in power that night and my dear church family readily responded to the challenge. We began to pray much more as a church. We saturated our worship services with prayer. We started a men's prayer meeting that met at 5:30 A.M. each Tuesday. Our ladies began to come together to pray. Our Sunday school classes began to seek the Lord in earnest. God was working out the same process in our church life that He was accomplishing in my personal life—He was bringing us to the place of brokenness.

Thanks, But I Can Do It Myself

Through the sense of failure I experienced, God was bringing me to the end of self-sufficiency. Before I even came to my new place of ministry, I had begun to earnestly pray that He would use my life in a greater way than ever. Unknown to me, the church where God sent me had also been praying that He would use them in a supernatural way. God put us together and allowed circumstances to develop in such a way that He brought us to the end of our own resources. He kept on until all we had left was Him. And that's not a bad place to be!

We have all learned to rely on our own strategies for getting our needs met. The Bible calls this mechanism for servicing our own needs the *flesh*. Every person has developed his flesh-life in order to get what he wants out of life as much of the time as possible. Don't think of flesh as skin, but as personal *techniques* for meeting your own perceived needs, apart from Christ. Your flesh-life may not be defiant against God. Walking after the flesh is simply relying on your own ability instead of on God's resources. Don't think of the flesh as something that you naturally find repulsive. It may be very attractive and even look spiritual.

Paul said that Christians should place no confidence in the flesh. Then he describes his own flesh patterns:

> I also might have confidence in the flesh. If anyone else thinks he may have confidence in the flesh, I more so: circumcised the eighth day, of the stock of Israel, of the tribe of Benjamin, a Hebrew of the Hebrews; concerning the law, a Pharisee; concerning zeal, persecuting the church; concerning the righteousness which is in the law, blameless. But what things were gain to me, these I have counted loss for Christ" (Philippians 3:3-7).

If you want to talk about credentials, Paul had them. Yet he said that these enviable qualifications had not proven to be assets, but liabilities. How can natural abilities become liabilities? It happens when we rely on those abilities instead of on Christ. Our flesh develops it's own unique patterns because of factors that have influenced our lives. They might be connected to our talents, appearance, wealth, education, or countless other things that we rely on to get through life. Saul of Tarsus had his flesh-life wrapped up in a religious package. Many Christians do the same. It is not uncommon for a Christian to find his need for acceptance and approval to be met by what he does at church.

Remember that a synonym for flesh may be self-sufficiency. It is God's purpose to bring us to the place where we rest totally in the sufficiency of Christ within us in every situation. Yet we have all learned how to handle life's circumstances by what *we* do ourselves. Many Americans believe that God helps those who help themselves. And sadly, many Christians have spiritualized that same false philosophy and concluded that God will bless us as we "do our part." For much of my life, I dedicated *my* abilities and *my* efforts to God. I tried hard to do something for God. I often prayed, "Lord, bless my efforts as I serve You."

However, the New Testament model of a Christian is not one who dedicates his own work to God. Rather it is the story of God Himself doing the work through a person totally yielded to Him.

It would be bad enough if the worst thing said about self-sufficiency was that it had no spiritual value in the Christian life. However, that would leave the impression that self-sufficiency is inconsequential, which is not the case. Trying to do something for God may sound admirable, but it produces damaging consequences. Consider the man who is known as the father of faith. When Abraham heard that he and Sarah were going to have a son, they were really excited. As the years passed and Sarah still didn't conceive, they decided to help God fulfill His promise.

"Sarah," Abraham might have said, "I've been

thinking. God told me that we were going to have a son, but perhaps we've been looking at this thing the wrong way. Maybe we should do everything we know to do and then trust that God will do the rest."

"You know, I've been having similar thoughts, Abe. Maybe God is going to do this in a different way than we first understood. Have you considered that the promised child might come through our servant, Hagar?"

"Well, to tell the truth, that thought had crossed my mind, Sarah. After all, we have to do our part."

You know the rest of the story. Abraham did go to Hagar and she did conceive. However, Ishmael was not the son God had promised. The son of promise would come through Sarah, and it would happen on God's timing. Abraham and Sarah were sincere, but they really made a mess of things. They were trying to do something to help God. One result of their self-sufficiency is the ongoing conflict between the Arabs and the Jews. The descendants of Isaac and Ishmael are still at war, all because Abraham and Sarah thought that God would bless *their* efforts to help Him.

During my senior year of high school, I worked in a nursing home. A part of my responsibility was to lift men from their wheelchairs into their beds. One evening I went into a man's room to help him into bed. He weighed in at about 200 pounds against my 130 pounds. Although I was thin, I knew how to lift a patient. I had been taught how to position myself in front of the wheelchair and place my hands under his arms with my legs on each side of his knees. I would then lift the patient and swing him around to the bed and set him down. It usually worked well, but not this time. When I had Mr. Daniels up and about halfway between the chair and the bed, he decided to "help" me. His intent was to stand up, but that's not what happened. Instead, he stiffened his whole body like a wooden plank. His feet shot out in front of him and he began to struggle. "Relax!" I told him. "I'm holding your weight. Just let me do it." But he didn't trust me. In his effort to stand up, he pulled himself away from my grip and fell to the floor. To make matters worse, he whacked me with the cane hanging on his chair! I tried to warm up to him in the days that followed, but he never would let me get too close to him again. There wouldn't have been a problem if he just hadn't tried to help.

Self-sufficient living always produces conflict. I know now that Melanie was right. I never would have been satisfied with life if the focus of my Christian experience had remained on doing what I believed was necessary to please God. I experienced peace only after I learned to focus on the person of Christ, instead of on what I should be doing for Him.

Are you struggling in your spiritual life? In order to experience genuine peace, it is necessary to come to the place where you no longer rely on your self-sufficient techniques and patterns. You probably won't give up easily, because you have relied on those resources all your life. So God may allow the weight of adverse circumstances to become greater than the strength of your flesh. And when this happens, it will hurt!

Don't Tell Me That God Won't Put More on Me Than I Can Bear!

You have probably heard all your life that God won't put any burden on you greater than you can bear. Don't mark me off as a heretic just yet, but I don't believe it. I believe that God *will* put heavier burdens on you than you can bear, especially when He is trying to bring you to the place of brokenness. God will allow the burden to be greater than you can bear so that you will finally allow *Him* to bear it for you. God's purpose in the breaking process is to bring you to the end of your own resources so that you will be ready to understand that He is the only resource you need in life. As long as your own abilities are sufficient to rise to the challenge, you will never understand that He doesn't just give strength. He *is* your Strength. In the breaking process, God has no intention of helping you *get* stronger. He wants you to become so weak that *He* can express Himself as the strength you need in every situation.

If you have prayed for God to use your life, don't be surprised when trouble comes. Remember, the trouble is intended to strip you of self-sufficiency, a necessary step before God can use you to the fullest. Many times I prayed for God to help with my circumstances and wondered why things didn't seem to get any better. In retrospect, I can see that God was helping by allowing things to get darker. I wanted Him to change the circumstances. He wanted to accomplish His purpose in the circumstance. When you pray for God to help with your situation and things don't get any better, remember that *He knows what He is doing*! Just because you can't see His hand doesn't mean He isn't working. He may be using the situation to break that outer shell of self-reliance that keeps the life of Christ from being expressed through your lifestyle. No Christian can ever live to full potential until that happens. As Watchman Nee says:

We must know that he who can work for God is the one whose inward man can be released. The basic difficulty of a servant of God lies in the failure of the inward man to break through the outward man. Therefore, we must recognize before God that the first difficulty to our work is not in others but in ourselves. Our spirit seems to be wrapped in a covering so that it cannot easily break forth. If we have never learned how to release our inward man by breaking through the outward man, we are not able to serve. Nothing can so hinder us as the outward man. Whether our works are fruitful or not depends upon whether our outward man has been broken by the Lord so that the inward man can pass through the brokenness and come forth. This is the basic problem. The Lord wants to break our outward man in order that the inward man may have a way out. When the inward man is released, both unbelievers and Christians will be blessed.[1]

While this breaking process is painful, it cannot be avoided if a Christian is to experience maximum usefulness in the ministry of Christ. As a pastor, I have seen a consistent flow of people who come through my office for counseling. I can't count the number of times when people who are experiencing pain in their lives have expressed this frustration: "I don't understand what is happening. I have asked God to use my life and I really meant it. But it seems like the more I try to do what He wants me to do, the harder things become."

Have you ever felt this way? Let's evaluate this expression of pain in light of the breaking process.

"I don't understand what is happening." We have all felt that way, haven't we? It is important to know that it is not necessary to always understand what is going on in our lives. The doctrine of God's sovereignty reminds us that He understands. Sometimes that is all we have to sustain us. However, many times there can be some understanding of what is happening when we hurt.

"I have asked God to use my life and I really meant it." Now this is where an understanding of our problems can begin to emerge. If we have sincerely asked God to use us, He will respond to that prayer. But we need to remember the truth about brokenness: God cannot use a Christian to fullest potential until that person has come to the end of confidence in personal abilities. So He allows problems to come into our lives which are greater than our abilities can solve. Don't miss this point because it is fundamental. If we have sincerely prayed for God to use us, He must cause us to come to the place where we have no confidence in the flesh. Adverse circumstances may be the hand of God working to bring us to the end of self-sufficiency.

"But it seems like the more I try to do what He wants me to do, the harder things become." Few of us want to live with adversity. Do you remember the definition already given for the flesh? Flesh refers to our self-effort to cope with life, relying on our own abilities. An unbroken Christian is accustomed to trying to live *for* God. He often rededicates himself to the Lord and determines to try to do what He wants.

God's purpose is not that we should rededicate our self with all its abilities, but that we should give up all hope in self. We sometimes try to live *for* Him when He wants to live His life *through* us. It is important to see the distinction here. To ask God to help us live for Him is to request some sort of divine blessing on our effort to "do what He wants us to do." But that isn't what God desires. He isn't interested in what we can do for Him. Christ is interested in living His life through us.

Is there a difference? You bet! It's the difference between law and grace. Law will cause a person to say, "Lord, help me to do the things You want me to do." In other words, "Help me keep Your rules." Grace will cause a person to say, "Lord Jesus, I am abiding in You and You in me. Express Your life through me in any way You desire." It isn't uncommon for Christians to think that God has a long list of things He wants His children to do. But in 1 Thessalonians 5:24 we read, "He who calls you is faithful, who also will do it." Not only does Christ call us to the Christian life, but He will also live it for us. After all, who else could live the Christ-life except Christ?

When God determines to bring us to brokenness so that Christ can live His life through us and we keep trying to live it ourselves, things will keep getting harder. When does it stop? When we reach the end of our self-sufficiency and have given up all hope in our own resources. Peter Lord has said, "Wouldn't it be awful to spend all your life trying to make God an apple pie, only to die and discover He never liked apple pie?"[2] God wants to bring us to the understanding that we weren't saved to do something for God. We were saved so that we might know Him in intimate daily fellowship. Do good works have a place in the Christian life? Of course! But they are an overflow of our relationship with Him, an evidence of His life being expressed through us.

Being preoccupied with serving Christ more than with Jesus Himself is a subtle threat to every Christian. Even one very close to Jesus during His earthly ministry fell into this trap. When Jesus came to visit Mary and Martha in their home at Bethany, Mary sat down at the feet of Jesus and listened intently to every word He spoke. Martha was busy doing things in the home to make His visit more enjoyable. Whether she was cooking or preparing His room, she felt uptight because company was in the house and she wanted to be a good hostess. As she hurried around, she couldn't help but notice Mary sitting there talking, while she was doing all the work.

> But Martha was distracted with much serving, and she approached Him and said, "Lord, do You not care that my sister has left me to serve alone? Therefore tell her to help me." And Jesus answered and said to her, "Martha, Martha, you are worried and troubled about many things. But one thing is needed, and Mary has chosen that good part, which will not be taken away from her." (Luke 10:40-42).

Martha was stressed out while Mary was resting. People for whom Christian living is strictly service-oriented often get impatient with those whose level of measurable activity is not as intense. Luke says that Martha was "distracted." Distracted from what? From Jesus! What was it that caused her attention to be distracted away from Jesus? You got it—serving Him! It was a startling revelation in my own life when the Holy Spirit showed me that I had become more preoccupied with the work of the ministry than with the One who called me to it. Busyness in serving Christ can block intimacy with Him.

Jesus could have said to Martha, "Now calm down. What you are doing is good, but what Mary is doing is important too. Both serving and resting have their proper place. Martha, you need to learn balance." Yet that isn't what He said. Instead, He said, "But one thing is needed and Mary has chosen that good part, which will not be taken away from her." How many things? *One* thing is needed—resting in Him. Does this statement minimize the importance of serving Jesus? Not at all. How do you suppose Mary would have responded if Jesus had asked her to bring Him a glass of water? She would immediately have sprung into action. On the other hand, if He had asked Martha for a glass of water, she might not have even heard Him because she was too busy making His bed—and He wasn't even sleepy! Do you see the point? Resting in Christ is the sole responsibility of the Christian. Everything else flows out of that.

Frank came into my office one morning before church. "Steve, I need to talk to you. Lately, I've been miserable. I teach Sunday school; I'm a deacon in the church; I sing in the choir; I serve on the finance committee. I'm doing everything I know to do for God, but I'm still unhappy. What's wrong with me?" Having just looked at Mary and Martha, what would you say might be his problem? Frank felt like Martha, worried and troubled about many things. Busy, but unfulfilled. I've been there, haven't you? Does it ever seem that the more you try to live for God, the harder things become?

I too had been busy trying to serve God, and I was frustrated and anxious. In fact, when I lay on the floor of my office crying in misery, it felt like hell. But I can look back now and see that God was getting me ready to experience a taste of heaven on earth.

CHAPTER 3

A BRAND
NEW ME

hen I was a student in high school, a hypnotist came to our science class. He brought four students to the front of the room and hypnotized them together. While they were in a trance he told them that when they woke up, they would each be an animal. One boy was told that he would be a monkey. Another would wake up as a dog. One girl would be a chicken and the other a turkey. The hypnotist said, "I will count to five and snap my fingers, and when I do you will wake up." He slowly counted to five, snapped his fingers, and they woke up like he had said.

What happened next was quite a sight. They behaved exactly like the animals they had been told they would become. One hopped around all stooped over, with his hands swinging by his sides like a monkey. He jumped up on a desk and screeched like Cheetah. The other boy started barking and running around the room like a dog. The chicken folded her hands under her arms and clucked as if she was trying to lay eggs.

The other girl strutted around like a turkey, gobbling as loud as she could and scratching at the floor with both hands. It was a comical sight to see people act like the animals they thought they were. After a while, the hypnotist woke them up and let them come back to their real identities. You can imagine how embarrassed they were when we told them how they had behaved.

Many Christians behave in ways that they don't understand. They want to be saints, but most of the time it seems that living like saints demands too much effort and attention. It is usually much easier just to "be yourself." Be yourself. That thought raises an important question. Who *are* you? For many years I didn't really know who I was. I knew that I had trusted Christ when I was eight years old and that I was going to heaven. But I lived my life under an assumed identity. It was a false identity that I accepted because of the power of suggestion that came to me through the world, the flesh, and the devil. I knew that I was a Christian, but I really didn't understand just how much my identity had changed when I was saved. Maybe you have lived with the same misconceptions.

Understanding our identity is absolutely essential to our success in living the Christian life. No person can consistently behave in a way that is inconsistent with the way he perceives himself. Next to a knowledge of God, a knowledge of who we are is by far the most important truth we can possess.[1] If we believe we are a dog, nothing can keep us from barking. If we believe we are a monkey, all the evidence in the world can't make us behave like anything else. Through the power of suggestion many Christians have been deceived into believing that they are something other than what God has made them to be. Jesus said, "The truth will set you free." Our identity in Christ is one of the most liberating truths we will ever understand.

You Are a New Person!

Debra had spent the last hour reciting an inventory of deficiencies in her life. She had been overweight for most of her life and had been made to feel ugly. Tears came to her eyes as she told how she felt like a social misfit who talked too much. Her parents had made her feel stupid from the time she was a child, even now often criticizing her "poor judgment" in taking care of matters in her home. Her husband told her that she would probably feel better about herself if she just lost some weight. It seemed that everything in her life had programmed her to believe that she was inadequate.

It didn't take a counselor to understand why she felt that her spiritual life just didn't measure up to God's expectations. "I guess I'll never be a good Christian like other people," she said.

"Deb, if ten means total acceptance, how would you rate your acceptance with God on a scale of one to ten?" I asked.

"About a three," she responded. Over the next weeks we talked together about her answer. It was an important issue. How would *you* answer that question?

Those who believe that they aren't fully accepted by God will find it difficult to experience intimacy with Him. It's not easy to warm up to somebody if you think they don't particularly accept or approve of you. Haven't you ever found yourself beginning to dislike a person you sensed didn't particularly like you? Maybe they didn't say or do anything to cause you to think they didn't like you. You just *felt* it. Were you inclined to reach out to them in any way? It goes against the grain to want to develop a relationship with someone you think doesn't care for you. The same is true when the other Person is God. One of Satan's most effective tools is to cause Christians to feel that God frowns when He looks at them.

Most Christians seem to have a spiritual inferiority complex. In spite of the fact that God speaks very highly of His children, they have a low opinion of themselves. Their perception of their identity is that they have been forgiven for their sins and saved by God's grace, but that they are still basically just sinners who are trying with God's help to live the kind of lifestyle He wants them to live. Do you see yourself as a saved sinner who tries to serve God to the best of your ability? That's how I understood my identity for much of my Christian life. But that description of the Christian falls far short of God's perception of those who have come to Him through Christ.

What does the identity of these people have in common? Michael Jordan is an athlete. Steve Martin is a comedian. Whitney Houston is a singer. Do you see a common denominator? The public identity of all three is based on their *behavior*. It's not only famous people who are identified by what they do. If someone asks you today, "Who are you?" what will you answer? I'm sure you'll tell them your name. But if they then ask, "Tell me about yourself," whatever you say next will probably reveal where you gain your sense of identity. And if you're like most folks, you will tell them about things you *do*. We've been programmed to think of identity as inseparable from behavior. But God doesn't look at it that way. He doesn't determine identity by behavior but by *birth*.

A person born into the family of God receives a

new identity. "Therefore, if anyone is in Christ, he is a new creation; old things have passed away; behold, all things have become new" (2 Corinthians 5:17). Paul says that those who have trusted Christ have become a *new* creation. The root of the word "creation" is "create." The word doesn't mean to improve something already in existence. It means to bring something out of nothing. God didn't simply change you when you were saved. He created a new person! You aren't the same person you were before you became a Christian.

Meet the New You

The person who was born when you trusted Christ is a *spiritual* being. Like God, man is a triune being. God exists in three persons while you consist of three parts: body, soul, and spirit. Your *body* has a sense consciousness which responds to the five natural senses. Your *soul* consists of mind, will, and emotions. Another word for soul is *personality*. The soul is self-conscious. Your spirit was dead when you were born into this world and remained that way until the Holy Spirit gave it life through the new-birth experience. The essence of your identity rests in your spirit. Someone has said that a person *is* a spirit who has a soul and lives in a body.

Before you trusted Christ you had no spiritual identity. That is why unsaved people struggle so hard to make a mark in this world. They are hungry for an identity. But a satisfying identity can never be found at the level of the soul or body. Since the essence of what we *are* is found at the spirit level, those outside of Christ are considered dead and those in Christ have been made alive. Paul said that God has brought to life those who were dead in their trespasses and sins (Ephesians 2:1).

What is the source that gives life to the spirit? It is nothing less than Christ Himself! When one turns to Him in repentance and faith, His Spirit comes into that person's spirit and gives life. Since it is the presence of Jesus in the spirit that gives it life, our identity is simply that we are *in Christ*! He becomes our life. "For in Him we live and move and have our being, as also some of your own poets have said, 'For we are also His offspring'" (Acts 17:28).

Living, moving, having our existence—that pretty much describes life. And the Bible says that for the believer it all takes place *in Him*. In Colossians 3:4 we read that Christ *is* our life! If Jesus is at the core of our existence, that gives us an identity much greater than most Christians acknowledge!

Consider some of the thrilling family traits that you received by being born into God's family and being placed into Christ:

• *You are a saint.* In 1 Corinthians 1:2, Paul addresses the people of the church at Corinth as saints. He certainly had to be talking about an identity which stemmed from their spiritual birth, because their behavior surely wasn't saintly. He calls them saints in chapter 1 and then spends the rest of his letter telling them to live like the saints they really are. Don't be uncomfortable with being called a saint, because that's what God calls you! That doesn't mean you live a sinless life, but that God has set you apart and placed the nature of Christ within you.

• *You are God's work of art.* "We are His workmanship, created in Christ Jesus" (Ephesians 2:10). The word "workmanship" is the Greek word *poema*, from which we get the English word "poem." God has made you to be a heavenly piece of poetry on this earth!

• *You are righteous and holy.* You have received the gift of righteousness (Romans 5:17). The Lord Jesus *is* your righteousness. When you received Him, your spirit was filled with righteousness. What you are at the spirit level determines your real identity. When you do not behave righteously, you are being inconsistent with who you are.

• *You are fully accepted by God.* You are accepted because you are *in Christ* (Ephesians 1:6). Because Christ has received you and He is fully accepted by the Father, you are fully accepted as well! You don't need to change a thing about yourself for God to accept you. Your acceptance isn't based on what you do, but on who you are.

These are just the tip of the iceberg! You may be thinking, "But I don't *feel* like a saint. I don't think of myself as a heavenly poem. I sure don't act very righteous and holy. I don't feel accepted by God." I know how you feel. But you must decide whether you are going to trust what you feel or what God has said in His word. Satan has caused many Christians to *believe* that they are not really new persons in Christ. He tells them that they should try to *act* like new creations because that is their Christian duty.

But that is not at all what God says. He says that you *are* a new creation. When you come to believe that fact by faith, you won't feel the need to act. You can just be yourself, allowing the nature of Christ within your spirit to flow through your personality and out of your life, like the river of living water that Jesus talked about that flows from one's innermost being.

Then Why Don't I Act Like Who I Am?

Remember the people who acted like animals when they were hypnotized? They acted that way because they temporarily believed a lie about their identity. When they were brought out of the hypnotic trance and understood reality, they began to behave like the people they really were.

Why do people who *are* holy act unholy? Why do many Christians struggle with sins, constantly trying to overcome them? It is because they have believed a lie! Satan, the great deceiver, has caused them to believe that at the core of their being, they are nothing more than rotten sinners. That describes what they were before they were saved, but not anymore!

If the hypnotist had been able to keep those four folks believing his suggestion, they would still be barking, cackling, gobbling, and screeching! But they did wake up to the truth. That's what needs to happen to many Christians today.

Have you been hypnotized to live under a false identity, so that you see yourself as nothing more than a saved sinner trying to serve God? Let this truth wake you up! You are not just a sinner saved by grace. You are a saint who has the life of Christ at the center of your being. A sinner saved by grace spends his time on the defensive against Satan. Someone who knows he is a saint goes on the offensive.

Bob George shares a great illustration of this truth. Imagine that a king decreed that a pardon would be extended to all prostitutes. Would that be good news for you if you were a prostitute? Of course, it would. You wouldn't have to worry any more about avoiding the law, or about having a criminal record. The pardon would definitely be good news to you. But it wouldn't necessarily give you the motivation to change your lifestyle.

But suppose that in addition to extending the pardon, the king came to you personally and asked you to become his wife. Would *that* give you a reason to change the way you live? Absolutely! Who wouldn't trade the life of a prostitute for that of a queen? Gaining a new identity as the king's wife would be your motivation to abandon prostitution.

When you became a Christian, you probably understood that all your sins were forgiven. But did that forgiveness give you sufficient motivation to change your behavior? The Bible says that we are the bride of Christ, and that relationship gives us a new identity![2] A proper understanding of our identity in Christ *is* sufficient motivation to have a totally different attitude toward sin.

Back to the four people who were hypnotized. When they woke up and realized how they had behaved, they felt pretty silly. That pictures the attitude of Christians who wake up to their true identity in Christ. They will sometimes lapse into old patterns of living and will choose to sin. But when they do, they *know* that their behavior is inconsistent with who they are. Their conduct contradicts their character. And it won't be long until they open their eyes and realize, "It's ridiculous for me to behave this way!"

It is important to see yourself as God sees you. You know how a caterpillar becomes a butterfly through the process of metamorphosis. The caterpillar weaves a cocoon around itself and a short time later emerges as a butterfly.

If you were to see a butterfly, it would never occur to you to say, "Hey, everybody! Come look at this good-looking converted worm!" Why not? After all, it was a worm. And it was "converted." No, now it is a new creature, and you don't think of it in terms of what it was. You see it as it is now—a butterfly.

In exactly the same way, God sees you as His new creature in Christ. Although you might not always act like a good butterfly— you might land on things you shouldn't, or forget you are a butterfly and crawl around with your old worm buddies—the truth of the matter is, you are never going to be a worm again![3]

It was within weeks after I experienced my emotional crisis that God began to teach me about my identity in Christ. It was liberating to understand just how He had made me into a butterfly. I was no longer a worm! In no way do I intend to convey the idea that understanding my identity caused me to live sinlessly. However, I have found that when I do sin now, I soon see it as foolish because I know that a sinful attitude or action contradicts my new nature. Before understanding my identity in Christ, I experienced condemnation when I sinned. Yet the Bible says there is no condemnation to those who are in Christ Jesus. All the condemnation of God against our sin was poured out on Jesus. So now I don't feel condemned, but am simply made aware by the Holy Spirit of the foolishness of what I have done. I am reminded of my identity in Christ and sense a *desire* to forsake the sin and get on with living like who I really am—a totally forgiven, fully accepted, redeemed saint!

If you have trouble thinking of yourself as a saint, you need to renew your mind through the Word of God. Renowned preacher Harry Ironside was once talking with someone about famous people in history who had been officially recognized as saints. Ironside asked him, "Have you ever met a real saint?"

"Oh no!" he responded. "But what a thrill that would be!"

"Glad to meet you," Ironside answered, as he stuck out his hand toward the man. "I'm Saint Harry." He was right. The New Testament refers to Christians as saints 63 times. Are you going to believe that fact or reject it? You *were* a sinner, separated from God. But now you *are* a saint! Just say out loud, "I am a saint." Did your mouth draw to one side as if you were about to have a stroke? Well, keep saying it until it feels comfortable. Believe the truth of God's Word. You *are* a saint!

A Butterfly Who Lived Like a Worm

There is a story in the Old Testament which clearly illustrates that God recognizes our identity by our spiritual birth and not by our behavior. Abraham had a nephew named Lot, who left Ur of the Chaldees along with his uncle when God led Abraham out. Young Lot was a fairly wealthy man. The Bible says that he possessed flocks, herds, and tents. As they traveled together, conflict began to develop between Abraham's herdsmen and those who tended to Lot's herds. Finally, Abraham came to Lot and suggested that they go separate ways in order to keep peace. He gave Lot the choice of location.

"And Lot lifted his eyes and saw all the plain of Jordan, that it was well watered everywhere (before the LORD destroyed Sodom and Gomorrah) like the garden of the LORD, like the land of Egypt as you go toward Zoar. Then Lot chose for himself all the plain of Jordan, and Lot journeyed east. And they separated from each other." (Genesis 13:10-11).

Lot took his family, herdsmen, and possessions and moved into Sodom. His decision was made purely on the basis of what he thought would benefit him financially. That was a major mistake.

Every mention of Lot living in Sodom indicates that he and his family became a part of that culture and blended right in. Lot's lifestyle certainly didn't indicate that he was anything other than a self-serving person. One glimpse of the depth of his sins in Sodom is mentioned in Genesis 19:36 where we read that both the daughters of Lot were with child by their father. But in spite of his behavior, God spoke to him in Genesis 19 and told him to get his family out of Sodom because He was about to destroy Sodom and Gomorrah. However, Lot's family didn't take this seriously. It seemed strange to them to hear talk of God's judgment coming from Lot's lips. His wife and daughters had to literally be taken by the hand and pulled out of the city, just before God destroyed it with fire and brimstone. You know how Lot's wife looked back and turned into a pillar of salt.

What word would *you* use to describe this man? Do you know how God thinks of him? God "delivered *righteous* Lot, who was oppressed by the filthy conduct of the wicked (for that *righteous* man, dwelling among them, tormented his *righteous* soul from day to day by seeing and hearing their lawless deeds)" (2 Peter 2:7-8, emphasis mine).

Huh? Are we talking about the same man? There's no doubt about it. *How* could God call this man righteous? In the Old Testament, God responded to the faith of believers by *imputing* righteousness to them. In Romans 4:3 we see that God "counted" (literally *imputed*) righteousness to Abraham because of his faith. Righteousness was *credited* to Lot because God saw faith in his heart, in spite of his contradictory actions.

Does this justify sinful behavior? Absolutely not! Ask Lot when you get to heaven if his sins were worth it, and I guarantee you he will tell you that his behavior was *foolish!* He didn't behave like the person he was.

Let's give Lot a little mercy; after all, God showed him great mercy. He *did* live in Old Testament times. He didn't have Christ living inside him as Christians do today. There is a big difference between Lot and believers today. God only *imputed* righteousness to Old Testament saints, but He *imparted* righteousness to you when you were saved. Imputing righteousness was a legal verdict, but imparting righteousness is a literal event that happens to New Testament saints. In these days of grace, Christians are literally given the righteousness of Christ. Lot had righteousness *credited* to him, but you had righteousness *created* in you when you were saved. Don't believe the lie that you are a worm. You are a butterfly. You are free to make the same kind of foolish choices that Lot made, but why would you want to do that? Remember who you are! Your identity is determined by your birth, not your behavior. Why would a butterfly want to crawl in the mud?

When God revealed my identity in Christ to me, it absolutely thrilled me. For the first time in my Christian life, I saw myself as He saw me. Have you reached that place in your life? But if the person you are now is a *new* you, what happened to the old you? The answer to that is one of the most exciting parts of this story.

CHAPTER 4

A DEAD OLD MAN

S ome of these stories preachers tell to illustrate a point should never have gotten started. Perhaps you have heard the one about the bulldog and terrier who fought every time they were together. The bulldog was strong because he was consistently well fed, while the terrier was weak because he rarely ate. So every time the dogs fought, the bulldog would emerge the winner. What would you need to do if you wanted to guarantee that the terrier would always win and the bulldog would always lose? You could feed the terrier and starve the bulldog. Eventually the terrier would become stronger and the bulldog would become weaker.

The point usually made with this story is that Christians possess an old and a new nature. These two natures are supposedly in conflict with each other all the time. If you want the terrier within you (your new nature) to win over the bulldog (your old nature), you need to feed the new nature and starve the old one.

There's just one problem with this story—it

illustrates a lie. That's right. It presents a lie that will absolutely enslave those who believe and act on its message. What this illustration fails to tell you is that the bulldog is dead. He was killed.

When God began to teach me about my identity in Christ, the truth about the death of my old nature was the most difficult thing for me to accept. Even when confronted with Scripture which clearly shows that the old nature was crucified with Christ, I thought that my old nature *felt* very much alive. But the truth is that the old Steve—the person I was before I was saved—is dead. I really wrestled with this fact. And even when God revealed the truth to me, I couldn't understand *how* it could be true. I felt like the boxer who went into the ring against a towering opponent. During every round, his opponent would pound him mercilessly. When the bell rang at the end of each round, he would return to his corner where his trainer would say, "Get out there and kill him! He hasn't laid a hand on you." This happened every round. "He hasn't laid a hand on you." Finally the boxer told his trainer, "Then you had better watch the referee, because *somebody* is beating the devil out of me!"

I know the feeling, don't you? When the Lord revealed the death of my old nature to me, I was confused. I knew somebody had been beating the devil out of me. A later chapter will discuss the issue of *the flesh* and its constant attack against the Christian. But for now, let's take a look at this issue of the old nature. What you believe about your nature may be the single greatest factor in determining the level of spiritual victory you experience.

What Is Your Nature?

Webster's defines *nature* as "the essential character of something; inborn character or disposition."[1] What is the essential, inborn character of the Christian? At the core of your life, at the spirit level, you have a disposition that hungers to glorify God.

Tony had come to talk about his relapse during his spring break from college. "I trusted Christ and was born again last year, but I'm still struggling at times with the temptation to smoke pot." He explained how he "kind of fell backward" during his recent trip to Daytona Beach with some college buddies. "Sometimes I wonder if I've really changed," he said.

"Tony, how do you feel right now about having smoked marijuana?" I asked him.

"Miserable," he quietly answered, his eyes staring at the floor. "Did you feel bad about smoking pot before you became a Christian?" I continued.

"Not really," he said. "I always said I wasn't hurting anybody with it."

"Do you know *why* you feel miserable now? It's because you are a new man. It isn't your nature to enjoy drugs anymore. The old Tony might have been a party animal who loved drugs. But that lifestyle contradicts the nature of the new Tony."

The *pleasure* of sinning doesn't disappear when a person trusts Christ. But after the short-lived pleasure is gone, sin leaves a Christian feeling empty and unfulfilled. Have you found that to be true when you sin? It isn't your nature now to live a lifestyle of sin. If this weren't true, you wouldn't experience inner conflict when you sin. If your basic nature was a sin nature, it wouldn't bother you to sin. It would be as comfortable for you as barking is for a dog or gobbling is for a turkey. However you're not comfortable with sin because your nature is not what it used to be. The new you has Jesus as your source of life. The old you was dead in sin. Before you were saved, you had one nature. It was the sin nature, sometimes called an unregenerate nature, the Adamic nature, the natural man, or your old self. The essence of your existence at that point is that you lived *in Adam*. You were totally dead to God. Since you trusted Christ, you still have only one nature, but it is not grounded in Adam. In fact, you are now dead to Adam. You are *in Christ* and your nature is the disposition of Jesus Himself! In 2 Peter 1:4, we read that we have become "partakers of the divine nature." That is the only nature the Christian possesses.

> Please understand that God had no plan for joining His Holy Spirit to any person's old sin nature. He had no plan to give birth to spiritual Siamese twins who are half spirit-child of Satan through Adam and half spirit-child of God through Christ. Jesus said, "Any city or house divided against itself shall not stand" (Matthew 12:25). God would never set you up for guaranteed failure by making you a "house divided against yourself." I'll agree that my experience and my feelings at times "tell" me I am a house divided, but since God would never set me up for certain failure, I must search His word to find another cause for my strife within. I am not a house divided.[2]

You don't have two natures. The only nature any

Christian has is the nature of the Lord Jesus Himself. Then what happened to the person we used to be?

The Old Man Died!

Paul often used the phrase "the old man" to describe the old sin nature that gave us our identity before we were saved. Since we have only one nature now, the nature of Christ Jesus, the question arises as to what happened to our old man. Look again at 2 Corinthians 5:17, "Therefore, if anyone is in Christ, he is a new creation; old things have passed away; behold, all things have become new."

We have already discovered that God created a *new* person when we trusted Christ as our Savior. So what happened to the old man? Paul says that the old has "passed away." You know what it means when someone has "passed away." To put it plain, they're dead. That's what happened to our old sin nature. It passed away and is never coming back. Maybe you haven't believed that your old sin nature is dead. But just for a moment, ask yourself this question: *Wouldn't it be wonderful if my sin nature was honestly dead?* This is where things get exciting because the Bible shows that our sin nature *is* dead!

Crucified With Christ

"I have been crucified with Christ; it is no longer I who live, but Christ lives in me; and the life which I now live in the flesh I live by faith in the Son of God, who loved me and gave Himself for me" (Galatians 2:20).

When Paul said that he had "been crucified with Christ," he spoke of a past event. The Greek word translated "crucified" is in the aorist tense, indicating that it was a historical event that took place at a particular time. He went on to say, "It is no longer I who live." There is an unavoidable truth in this verse. We have been put to death with Jesus Christ on the cross and do not live anymore.

Who was Paul speaking about when he said, "*I* have been crucified and *I* no longer live?" He was referring to his sin nature. Our sin nature died with Jesus Christ on the cross almost 2,000 years ago. If you have trouble accepting that fact, then consider this question: *If it wasn't our sin nature that died, what did die?* Paul teaches here that the old self is forever dead. Our sin nature won't be coming back. The life we now possess is nothing less than the very life of Jesus Christ!

We Died to Sin!

How shall we who died to sin live any longer in it? Or do you not know that as many of us as were baptized into Christ Jesus were baptized into His death?

Knowing this, that our old man was crucified with Him, that the body of sin might be done away with, that we should no longer be slaves of sin. For he who has died has been freed from sin. Now if we died with Christ, we believe that we shall also live with Him (Romans 6:2-3,6-8).

Look at the number of times these verses say that *we* died with Christ. What part of us died? Our old man—that sin nature we possessed before we were saved. D. Martyn Lloyd-Jones commented on these verses from Romans 6:

> This is, to me, one of the most comforting and assuring and glorious aspects of our faith. We are never called to crucify our old man. Why? Because it has already happened—the old man was crucified with Christ on the cross. Nowhere does the Scripture call upon you to crucify your old man; nowhere does the Scripture tell you to get rid of your old man, for the obvious reason that he has already gone. Not to realize this is to allow the devil to fool you and to delude you. What you and I are called upon to do is to cease to live as if we were still in Adam. Understand that the "old man" is not there. The only way to stop living as if he were still there is to realize that he is not there. That is the New Testament method of teaching sanctification. The whole trouble with us, says the New Testament, is that we do not realize what we are, that we still go on thinking we are the old man, and go on trying to do things to the old man. That has been done; the old man was crucified with Christ. He is non-existent, he is no longer there. If you are a Christian, the man that you were in Adam has gone out of existence; he has no reality at all; you are in Christ.[3]

The Old Life Was Taken Away

"In Him you were also circumcised with the circumcision made without hands, by putting off the body of the sins of the flesh, by the circumcision of Christ" (Colossians 2:11). God established circumcision as a sign of His covenant with the Hebrew people. The removal of the foreskin of every male was an evidence of the removal of their old identity and of their newly acquired covenant relationship to God. But Paul suggests that in these days of grace, God has established a new covenant with His people. Under this new testament, the circumcision will involve the inner man, not the outer man. Charles Stanley says about this verse:

> [God] uses circumcision to illustrate cutting away that part of the body by which life is generated. What he is saying is that God cut away—He took away that old sinful nature we received from our parents. That nature that has been poisoned by the Adamic nature. That old sin nature is that within us which causes us to disobey and rebel. God deals with that in salvation. God has taken away from us that which was given at birth—that old sinful nature. Someone will say, "Do you mean to tell me that my old sinful nature with which I was born has been taken away?" It has been taken away. That is what he is referring to when he speaks of circumcision, that cutting away.[4]

So the source of our old life has been cut away from us forever by the circumcision performed on us by the Spirit of God. God didn't clear out the cobwebs; He killed the spider! When we sin we are acting in a way that is *unnatural* for us. Our conduct contradicts our character when we sin. That's why Paul says, "Set your mind on things above, not on things on the earth. For, *you died*, and your life is hidden with Christ in God" (Colossians 3:2-3, emphasis mine). The old you is dead!

But I Don't Feel Dead

Feelings can really deceive a person. Last year our family went to Six Flags Over Georgia several times. On one of those visits, I allowed myself to be talked into getting on a ride called the Freefall. It's a ride designed for feeble-minded folks who have no better sense than to climb into a small seat like those on a Ferris wheel, be strapped down, lifted ten stories into the air, and then be dropped. I gave in to the pressure and found myself waiting in line to experience this kind of "fun." An interesting thing happened to me when I sat down on that seat and a young man began to strap me in. My feelings began to talk to me—no, I take that back—they began to yell at me. In one unified voice they screamed, "You're going to die! You're going to die!" And do you know, for a moment I believed my feelings! But just before the moment when my life would have passed before my eyes, I got a grip on my feelings. In a way, I answered them back. "No, I'm not going to die. I stood here and watched dozens of people ride this thing ahead of me and they didn't die. This ride has been here for years and nobody has ever died riding the Freefall. An engineer designed this thing. It has been regularly inspected. It is safe. No, I definitely won't die." My feelings responded, "Well then, you're going to *really* hurt your back!" This all happened within the few seconds between being strapped in and falling. My feelings lied. I didn't die and didn't even hurt my back. It was so much fun that it will last me a lifetime. In other words, I'll never do it again.

As I thought about the incident later, it was amusing to me that a man my age could get that nervous (that sounds better than "scared") about an amusement park ride. It's tough to act on facts when feelings are screaming something that contradicts the truth. Yet we face that kind of choice many times in our Christian experience. You may be facing that kind of situation right now with this truth about your old nature. If you don't *feel* as if your sin nature is dead, you may be tempted to reject this truth. But if you don't accept it, what are you going to do with the verses that clearly teach that we died with Christ? While it may go against your feelings, the truth is that a Christian has only one nature.

Jesus made this very clear, and the body of Scripture documents it. He said you couldn't sew a patch of new cloth on an old garment. He meant this as an analogy of the new man and the old man. It's futile to try to join them together, and God did not make a lie of Jesus' teaching. Jesus said you can't put new wine (the Holy Spirit) into old skins (the old nature), because the old skins can't contain the glory of His presence. You've got to put the new wine into new skins (new nature).

The Scriptures likewise say that you cannot join light (Holy Spirit) with darkness (old man). The Word further says that a believer (live-spirit child of God) must never join himself in marriage to an unbeliever (dead-spirit child of Satan). We know He would never violate His own admonition by joining into union the old man and the new man inside your earthsuit.

Jesus said, "No one can serve two masters" (Matthew 6:24). Now I ask you, would God who taught all the foregoing truths deliberately "set up" the Christian by giving him two conflicting identities, one loyal to God, the other equally loyal to Satan? No! Lost people have one master (Satan), not two. Christians also have one master (God), not two.[5]

You may not *feel* that your sin nature is dead, but God says that it is. This in no way means that you will live a life of sinless perfection. It does mean that it is not your nature to live a life of habitual sin anymore. The conflict between flesh and spirit will exist as long as you are in this world. However, saints have the freedom to choose to sin or not to sin. By the life of Christ the new you has the desire to resist sin and the power to live victoriously.

Within days after that night of absolute surrender in my office, God began to reveal the truths of my identity in Christ. I understood that when I was saved, He had given me a new nature. For the first time I knew that my old man really was dead. But the time came when the process moved from the theological and academic realm into practical experience. Head knowledge alone wasn't enough to experience victory. Just like a man who understands the gospel intellectually and then finally receives Christ, so I came to the place where *learned* truths became *living* truths to me. It became apparent that God didn't want to *change* my life as I had asked—He wanted to *exchange* it.

CHAPTER 5

EXPERIENCING HIS LIFE

It didn't take a second thought for me to decide how to respond to the letter I held in my hand. Just a few weeks earlier, when I lay on the floor in my office, I surrendered myself to God. I chose to empty myself before Him. I asked Him to put back into me anything that He wanted there. For the past few weeks, things had seemed sort of strange. I felt like I was drifting in a theological sea where I didn't know what to hold onto anymore. I knew that the "buckle down and do something for God" mentality that I had lived with prior to the experience of absolute surrender wasn't right. Now I didn't know how to approach ministry. I wasn't even sure how to approach the Christian life. I had finally discovered that trying hard to experience victory just didn't work. But what was the answer? I had been praying every day for the Lord to show me the way.

The letter I held struck a chord in me. A pastor was inviting me to a one-day seminar sponsored by Grace Ministries International.[1] In the letter, the pastor spoke about how the truths taught at a prior conference had revolutionized his life. I had always admired his ministry and believed that anything that had so impacted his life could probably help me too. I had been to dozens of seminars over the years, and yet I had an inner sense that this would be different. And different it was.

As I attended the seminar, the truths taught soaked into me like water into parched ground. In the weeks that followed, I began to recognize my own flesh patterns and to see that my futile struggle for success in my church had been God's way of bringing me to the end of self-sufficiency. For the first time in my life, I began to really understand my identity as a Christian—that Christ is not simply *in* my life, but that He *is* my life.

One day as I sat at my desk in my office, I resigned my church. In fact, I resigned from trying to live a Christian life. *Lord Jesus,* I prayed, *I know now that I've gone about trying to live my whole life the wrong way. I have tried and tried to live for You—to make my mark on this world for You. I have tried, with Your help, to do a work for You in the churches I have served. But today, Lord, I quit. I am not going to try anymore. I understand now that You are my very life. So whatever needs to be done, You will have to do it through me. I am going to rest in You and whatever happens—happens. You are my life.*

For weeks I lived on an emotional Mount Everest. I couldn't stop talking about this new life I was *experiencing.* I had possessed the life all the time, but now I was experiencing and enjoying what I had possessed from the day I was saved. I was like the pauper who discovered oil on the property where he had lived all his life. I would call Melanie on the telephone two or three times a day and excitedly read to her from *Lifetime*

Guarantee.[2] I would "feel a sermon coming on" and would call and preach it to her. She jokingly said that she thought I had been saved again. So did I. At least, it felt that way.

The exchanged life is not some second work of grace. It is a new awareness and appreciation for the first work of grace! I didn't get anything new from God when I prayed that prayer. Rather, I just began to *enjoy* what God had given me when I was born again as an eight-year-old boy. In a short time, Melanie too would come to understand the full meaning of Christ as her very life. Things haven't been the same for either of us since.

Don't assume that a euphoric mountaintop is necessary to validate the appropriation of Christ as your life. The effect that spiritual truth has on a person's emotions depends on their individual personality. Melanie came to appropriate Christ as life without the emotional explosion I experienced. For her, it was simple faith without the emotion. Yet the impact of understanding this truth has caused a transformation in her which is every bit as radical as what I have experienced. The key for us both was *faith*, not emotion. It would be unwise for any Christian to seek some kind of emotional confirmation when he appropriates Christ as his life. In any aspect of the Christian walk, feelings are incidental, not fundamental.

Christ Is Our Life

"His divine power has given to us all things that pertain to life and godliness, through the knowledge of Him who called us by glory and virtue, by which have been given to us exceedingly great and precious

> promises, that *through these you may be par-*
> *takers of the divine nature*, having escaped the
> corruption that is in the world through lust
> (2 Peter 1:3-4, emphasis mine).

The human spirit is the essence and core of our existence. Before we trusted Christ, we had no meaningful
identity because our spirit was dead. But when we
trusted Jesus Christ, the Spirit of Christ came into us
and we gained an identity grounded in Christ. Peter
said that we became partakers of the divine nature.
Since the Spirit of Christ comes into a person's spirit at
salvation, and because the essence of what we are is
determined at the spirit level, one who has trusted
Christ becomes a *Christian*.

To say that you are a Christian doesn't simply refer
to the particular set of doctrinal beliefs you hold. It
doesn't just refer to the way you live. It points to what
you *are* at the deepest level of your being. At the center of your being is Christ! He has become your very
life! "But he who is joined to the Lord is one spirit with
Him" (1 Corinthians 6:17). When you received Christ,
you were joined together with Him in an eternal
union. He now lives in you and desires to express His
life through you.

Someone has said that Jesus gave His life *for* us so
that He could give His life *to* us and live His life *through*
us. A believer has become one with Christ. As we rest
in Him, He will express Himself through our lifestyle.
The identity of the Christian isn't connected to his
place in this world, but stems from his relationship to
Christ! As Paul said, "And He died for all, that those
who live should live no longer for themselves, but for
Him who died for them and rose again. Therefore,

from now on, we regard no one according to the flesh"
(2 Corinthians 5:15-16a).

The totality of the Christian's life is contained in
Jesus Christ! The Christian life is not *about* Christ. It *is*
Christ. It is God's purpose to bring every Christian to
the place where he no longer lives for self, but where
Christ is allowed to live His life through us.

Shelly had just prayed to receive Christ. Like every
new Christian, she had a real desire to leave my office
with the confidence that she would *live* a Christian
lifestyle. She was the first person I had introduced
to Christ after I came to understand grace for the
Christian life. Before this time, I would have given her
a list of things that a new Christian ought to do in
order to "get started right." This time I took a different
approach. I didn't tell her all the "spiritual" things to
do. Instead, I told her that Christ was her life, and as
she would abide in Him, everything she would do
would be spiritual. I explained to her that the Holy
Spirit inside her would give her the *desire* to glorify
God. I stressed how her identity had changed in the
past few minutes. I showed her from Scripture how she
had become a partaker of the divine nature and had
become one with Christ. I encouraged her to simply
choose to live each moment allowing Christ to live His
life through her. Then she said something that thrilled
me. I had never heard a new Christian say it before. In
fact, it had taken me twenty-nine years of my Christian
life to discover it. *"The Christian life is easy, if you just let
Him do it."* She wasn't a seasoned Christian. She hadn't
even been baptized yet. Yet she saw it and said it out
loud. The Christian life is easy, if you just let Him do
it.

Why Can't I Live the Christian Life?

Do you look at the Christian life as being easy or hard? I spent many years repeatedly rededicating myself to the Lord. But no matter how much I wanted to live for Christ or how hard I tried, I continued in a cycle of inconsistency. I sincerely wanted to be consistent, but just couldn't. Can you relate to that experience? If so, I have some good and bad news for you. The bad news is this—*you will never be able to live the Christian life.* The harder you try, the more certain you are to fail. Trying will *always* lead to frustration and failure.

As a part of my pastoral responsibilities, I have visited many hospitals. On numerous occasions I have seen people on a respirator. I've watched people wake up on a breathing machine after open heart surgery. Certain people have real trouble with those machines. It's the people who *try* who run into trouble. The respirator is built to do the breathing. The patient just needs to relax. But when a person panics and tries to breathe, alarms beep and the patient is uncomfortable, because he is working against a machine designed to breathe for him. I've been told that it's a scary feeling.

Living the Christian life is similar to breathing. In fact, the Greek word translated "spirit" is the word *pneuma*, which can also be translated as "breath." (You have seen the root word in pneumonia and pneumatic.) God never intended for the Christian life to be a struggle. The Holy Spirit should flow from the life of the Christian as naturally as breathing. But many Christians are hyperventilating trying to do something for God.

That's the bad news, but here is the good news—

Christ will live His life through you. God never intended for you to live the Christian life—only Christ can live the Christ-life! He is willing to live it through you any time you will allow Him to do it!

Many modern church members are absolutely exhausted from their efforts to serve God. You had better be fit enough to run a marathon race if you become a part of some churches. It doesn't take long to discover the long-distance runners in a congregation. These folks will be called on to run till they drop. Don't misunderstand. There is nothing wrong with *spiritual service*, but *religious activity* isn't worth two cents. Many Christians have burned out because they have wrongly assumed that they must keep on keeping on, no matter how tired they are or how much they hate it. Many in the modern church are teaching their classes, singing in the choir, keeping the nursery, knocking on doors, making telephone calls, ad infinitum, because they believe it is their duty. Yet in spite of all they do, they are spiritually, emotionally, and physically tired. Their load is heavy, but they keep on because of their "commitment."

Does the previous paragraph describe you? Then look at what Jesus had to say about spiritual service:

> Come to Me, all you who labor and are heavy laden, and I will give you *rest*. Take My yoke upon you and learn from Me, for I am gentle and lowly in heart, and you will find *rest* for your souls. For My yoke is *easy* and My burden is *light* (Matthew 11:28-30, emphasis mine).

How do these words compare with the lifestyle of

many contemporary Christians? Jesus used words like "rest" and "easy" and "light" to describe the Christian life. If these words don't describe your lifestyle, you aren't experiencing the quality of Christian life that God intends. I'm not talking about your circumstances. I am referring to your spiritual perspective. If serving God makes you miserable, something is wrong! Why are many in the modern church exhausted? Why are so many Christians tired of trying unsuccessfully to live the Christian life? They have much in common with the folks who try to "help" the respirator. They are working against God's designed method of Christian living.

The Body of Christ

During His incarnate ministry, Jesus lived in a physical body. But at the ascension, His body was carried away by a cloud into heaven. Yet the New Testament clearly teaches that Jesus continues His ministry in the world today. Does He do it without a body? No. The Bible says that we are the body of Christ in the world today. Christ lives within us and desires to perform His ministry through us.

> Or do you not know that your body is the temple of the Holy Spirit who is in you, whom you have from God, and you are not your own? For you were bought at a price; therefore glorify God in your body and in your spirit, which are God's (1 Corinthians 6:19-20).

The Lord Jesus still has a body in the world today—it is His church! You are a part of the body of Christ, if the Spirit of Jesus lives inside you. God wants you to absolutely yield yourself to Him, allowing Christ not only to live in your body, but to express His life through you. Any spiritual service should be the result of the Spirit of Christ moving through you in ministry. It is *His* responsibility to do the work of Christian ministry. It is *your* responsibility to be absolutely surrendered to Him.

A real barrier preventing Christians from enjoying the rest that Jesus promised is self-effort. Many have been so conditioned to believe that they must "do something for God" that they are constantly struggling to do more and more. Many have rededicated *self* to God again and again. Yet self is what stands in the way of victorious Christian living. As long as *we* struggle to live the Christian life, Christ is hindered from living it through us. So, why do Christians continue to try to live the Christian life out of self-effort?

• *They don't know any other way.* Many Christians sincerely believe that all God asks is that they do their best to live for Him. It seems logical that God couldn't expect any more than that we do our best. This was the reason I did my best to live for God. However, doing our best to experience victory after we become Christians will be no more successful than doing our best to become a Christian.

• *They find fulfillment through self-effort.* While self-effort in the Christian life won't give spiritual rest or peace, it will often provide a sense of accomplishment that feeds one's ego. If a person feels that he can't experience spiritual victory, he may settle for the affirmation that comes with religious accomplishment.

However, there is a big difference between fulfillment and contentment. I experienced fulfillment in my life as a pastor many times through the years. When attendance was growing, I felt fulfilled. When people affirmed the messages I preached, I felt gratified. Any time the *results* of my work seemed to confirm the *value* of my efforts, I felt good about it. But the affirmation through positive results was never enough to bring contentment. I wanted *more* success. That's the problem with living from our own resources. Flesh can gratify but never really satisfy. Real satisfaction can come only from our relationship to Christ, not by what we do for Him. The old Rolling Stones song *I Can't Get No Satisfaction* could well be the signature song of many Christians who are propelled by self-effort. Even if they can't gain any spiritual mileage, they can sure rev up the religious RPMs! It is possible to be a superstar in your local church, in spite of the fact that your works mean absolutely nothing to God. Someone has rightly said, *God doesn't appreciate what He doesn't initiate.* However, other church members may greatly appreciate it.

• *They are motivated by guilt.* Many Christians live in constant shame, feeling that they aren't doing enough for God. Dawn grew up in a home where she was made to feel guilty about almost everything in her life. She said that the question she remembers being asked most often by her mother was, "Aren't you ashamed of yourself?" If she didn't eat all the food on her plate, she heard, "With all the starving people around the world, aren't you ashamed of yourself?" If she disobeyed her mother, it was, "After all I've done for you, aren't you ashamed of yourself?" Regardless of what she did right or wrong, she was hit with, "Aren't you ashamed?"

As an adult, she was a busy Christian but not a very happy one. In spite of all her religious activity, she still heard a phantom voice whispering, "Aren't you ashamed of yourself?" People like Dawn are consumed with what they think they *owe* God, and they spend their lives trying to do more. They miss the point that grace can never be repaid. It has no price, not because it is worthless, but because it is priceless. These people fail to understand that God can do anything He wants done. He doesn't want what you can *do*. Jesus said that apart from Him, you can do nothing. Instead, He wants *you*.

• *They hope to gain God's acceptance.* Some Christians believe that God's acceptance depends on how faithfully they serve Him. But God's love and acceptance are totally unconditional. I once actually heard a parent say to his son, "Now you be a good boy so the Lord will love you." Nothing could be further from the truth! A person's behavior has absolutely no influence on God's love. He loves you because, in His grace, He has *chosen* to do so. You can't do anything to gain God's acceptance, because Jesus has already done everything to cause the Father to accept you. You are fully accepted by God because you are in Christ. You can't improve on total acceptance, and God already accepts you totally. Yet there are believers who still struggle to do all the right things to cause God to love and accept them.

There may be other reasons why Christians try to live the Christian life out of self-effort. But one thing is sure—it takes divine action to bring a person to the place of renouncing self-sufficiency and beginning to rest in Christ's sufficiency. It's tough to let go of self-sufficiency after having lived a lifetime relying on it. God often works through a painful process to bring a person to the place of being willing to renounce the self-life.

Have you been struggling to live for God? Maybe God is bringing you to the place where you are willing to renounce your self-sufficiency and begin to rest in the fact that Christ is your life. It is painful to lay down *your* life in order to experience Christ's life. But remember these words of Jesus: "For whoever desires to save his life will lose it, but whoever loses his life for My sake will find it" (Matthew 16:25).

Jesus makes a tremendous offer to every person who will accept it. If you will give Him your life, He will give you His. What an exchange! Is your Christian life one of rest? Do you find the yoke of Christian service to be easy? Are your burdens light? The life of Jesus makes the Christian experience a real delight, not a religious duty.[3]

The link between the facts of the exchanged life and the *experience* is faith. Just as a person becomes a Christian through faith, so victory in the Christian life is realized through faith. Jesus Christ *is* your life. Appropriating the truths of the exchanged life is the necessary step to experiencing Christ as your life. For me, it occurred when I prayed the prayer at the beginning of this chapter. It's not the words that make the difference, but whether you are willing to formally renounce self (not rededicate it) and appropriate the truth of Christ as your life.

When I began to *experience* Christ as my life, I felt like a new Christian. I used to believe that the

Christian walk revolved around doing certain things and avoiding others. Now it was a matter of learning how to enjoy the freedom of grace.

CHAPTER 6

FREE FROM
THE LAW

ome time ago my wife wanted me to accompany her to the High Museum of Art in Atlanta. Knowing that I could stand some "cultural enrichment," I reluctantly agreed to go. After spending hours staring blankly at one-eyed portraits and twisted steel, we moved into an area filled with antiques. There we saw beautiful old pieces of furniture, on elevated platforms. As we approached the first one, I noticed a sign that read, "Do not stand on this platform." As I was stepping up onto the platform, I was thinking, "I know this thing will hold me." Immediately I realized what I had done and stepped back down. The sign forbidding me to stand on the platform provoked an immediate reflex to step up! It never would have occurred to me to stand on the platform if the sign hadn't forbidden it.

Many Christians focus on the laws of God. Their concept of victorious Christian living is to avoid wrong actions and do right ones. They often study God's Word, learning all the things they must stop and the things they must start. They are focused on the rules of the Christian life. They want to be told where they can stand and not stand and still be okay in the eyes of God. They believe that if they can only *do* the right things, they will grow spiritually and enjoy a victorious Christian walk.

However, any approach to Christian living that focuses on keeping rules as a means of experiencing victory or growing spiritually is *legalism*. Legalism is a system in which a person seeks to gain God's acceptance or blessings by what he does. People who live this way are called *legalists*. Can an unsaved person be a legalist? Of course. Is it possible for a Christian to be a legalist? Yes! Is your concept of the Christian life one which suggests that God's primary concern with you is your behavior? If so, you are a card-carrying member of the Legalist Lodge. God's concern with you isn't about rules but relationship. When you properly understand your relationship to God, the rules tend to take care of themselves. But when your focus is on the rules, spiritual failure is certain.

Don and Debra had struggled with consistency in their Christian life for a long time. One Sunday morning they said they had something they wanted to tell me. "We've come to an important decision. We believe that a big part of our problem has been our lack of involvement in church. So we have made a commitment to each other that during the coming year we are going to attend church every Sunday, no exceptions. That's the only way we are ever going to be able to get our lives straightened out. We will not miss church even once this year." I cringed on the inside as I listened. Don't get me wrong—every pastor wants to see his church members in attendance, but I knew that this kind of approach would eventually backfire. Don and Debra had been attending church about once a month. After their decision to come every Sunday, they attended three weeks in a row. Then they never came back. They finally joined a church closer to their house. They said it would be easier to be faithful in attendance if they didn't have to leave home so early on Sundays. They believed that if they could attend church often enough, that would make them spiritual. It is certainly good for Christians to attend church, but they turned church attendance into a self-imposed law. "We *must* attend church every Sunday." Then that law did what law always does—it stimulated rebellion.

First Corinthians 15:56 says that *the power of sin is the law* (NAS). Focusing on rules will never lead to obedience, but will stimulate a person to disobedience. Paul made this truth very clear.

> For when we were in the flesh, the sinful passions *which were aroused by the law* were at work in our members to bear fruit to death. But now we have been delivered from the law, having died to what we were held by, so that we should serve in the newness of the Spirit and not in the oldness of the letter (Romans 7:5-6, emphasis mine).

One reason for inconsistency in the life of many Christians is that they don't really understand that they are dead to the law. The law says, "You must, you ought," while grace causes a person to say, "I want to!" The Bible and Christian experience both validate that trying to live by a list of rules can never bring a lifestyle of victory. For many years I believed that to become a "good" Christian a person should do certain things such as attending church, reading the Bible, praying, witnessing to others about Christ, etc. These actions are an integral part of life for one who is expressing the life of Christ. But they should be the result of intimacy with Christ, not a *means* for achieving intimacy. Had Don and Debra *wanted* to attend church, nothing could have kept them away. Embracing a "must attend church" law was their expressway out the door.

Taking a disciplined approach in these matters didn't produce joy in my Christian life. Regardless of how much I did, I never felt as if it were enough. There have been periods of my life when I would arise very early in the morning to read the Bible and pray for extended periods of time. I would witness to everything that breathed. I would memorize passages of Scripture. I did everything I believed a Christian should do to please God, and yet it was never enough. I could never experience joy in Jesus because of my focus on the spiritual disciplines still undone. No matter how many spiritual miles I traveled, I always saw "ought to's" ahead of me stretching into the horizon. I seldom enjoyed the scenery along the way.

I never consistently knew *real* joy in those actions I considered to be spiritual disciplines until after I understood the truth of Christ as my life. For instance, I grew up reading the Bible every day. In fact, we received a slip of paper in a discipleship class on Sunday where we checked off whether or not we had read our Bible every day during the previous week. I gradually developed a mentality that emphasized how a Christian *ought* to read his Bible every day. My focus wasn't on the idea of *wanting* to read the Bible. I just knew I *ought* to read it every day. So for me, daily Bible reading became a law. It was something that I must do because God required it of good Christians. I can remember as a kid opening the Bible at night before I fell asleep and reading a verse just so I could check that box on Sunday. Years later I would read it so I could check the same box in my mind, saying I had done what was expected by God. I might not have a *desire* to read the Bible, but I had a *duty* to read it. I found it difficult to be consistent with my "quiet time." The self-imposed law which said I ought to do it stimulated a desire not to do it, just like Paul said in Romans 7:5! Yet at those times when I didn't read it, I felt condemnation because I didn't do what I "ought" to have done. So the law made me not want to read the Bible and then condemned me when I didn't!

It may sound strange, but I really began to enjoy the Bible when I realized that I didn't *have* to read it. From how much of the law has the Christian been set free? All of it! Is there a law that requires we read the Bible a certain amount of time each day? No! Then why read it? Because we have a *desire* to fellowship with God in His Word. A grace-oriented approach to Bible study creates a hunger for it, while a law-oriented approach makes it a tiresome task that must be done. When I was a legalist, I was *bound* and determined to read the Bible because I should. Now I am *free* to read it because it is what I want! I was not free to read the Bible until I discovered that I was free not to read it.

Legalism Without Life

If you have the impression that I am minimizing the place of the Bible in the life of the Christian, you are missing my point. I know the Bible speaks about the importance of feeding from God's Word daily.

However when a person's goal is simply to read the Bible, he isn't seeing the big picture. We should read the Bible because we want to know Christ in a more intimate way, not just to fulfill a religious duty.

Nobody in the New Testament was more committed to studying the Bible than the Pharisees. They could quote long passages from memory. They knew the content of their Bible because they poured over it daily. But Jesus had a word to say about their kind of Bible study, "You search the Scriptures, for in them you think you have eternal life; and these are they which testify of Me. But you are not willing to come to Me *that you may have life*" (John 5:39-40, emphasis mine).

Jesus was pointing out that their approach to the Bible was nothing more than an academic discipline. They *knew* their Bible, but there was no life in their empty religious routines.

Their approach to the Bible was no different than the approach some Christians today take toward the activity of their Christian life. There are people who attend church, preach sermons, teach Bible classes, sing, pray, tithe, and do a dozen other things that they believe God expects *without one ounce of spiritual life in what they are doing.* That may be church ministry, but can it really be called *Christian* ministry? What separates Christian ministry from empty religious activity? *Life!* Much activity takes place in the modern church that has no real life in it. Many Christians are trying hard to work for God in the church and finding absolutely no joy in it at all. They are focusing on *doing* all the right things, but are missing the life of Christ in what they do, because their perspective is based on law.

When a person builds his lifestyle around a long list

of things he thinks he ought to do, he will eventually
feel exhausted spiritually, emotionally, and even physically. Yet many keep pushing forward on a religious
treadmill, because it is what they believe God expects.
They know their church expects it. So they keep "serving" even though they feel miserable and empty. They
behave like prisoners of the law. They are bound to do
what they think they ought to do, mistakenly calling
this "the Christian life."

When our focus is on the things we *ought* to do, we
find ourselves struggling to be obedient. We feel bound
to do certain things. When we begin to experience
Christ as our *life* on a daily basis, all the matters of
Christian living which before were law now become a
natural expression and an overflow of His life. We
aren't bound to the law anymore. We died to the law
when our old nature was put to death with Christ. We
are now bound only to a person—the Lord Jesus. Paul
explains our freedom from the law:

> You know very well, my brothers (for I
> am speaking to those well acquainted with
> the subject), that the Law can only exercise
> authority over a man so long as he is alive. A
> married woman, for example, is bound by
> law to her husband so long as he is alive. But
> if he dies, then his legal claim over her disap-
> pears. This means that, if she should give her-
> self to another man while her husband is
> alive, she incurs the stigma of adultery. But if,
> after her husband's death, she does exactly
> the same thing, no one could call her an adul-
> teress, for the legal hold over her has been dis-
> solved by her husband's death...the death of

Christ on the cross has made you "dead" to
the claims of the law, and you are free to give
yourselves in marriage, so to speak, to another, the one who was raised from the dead,
that you may be productive for God (Romans 7:1-4, PHILLIPS).

The Christian is dead to the law! Our old self was
subject to the law, but we have already discovered in
chapter 4 that our old man—the person we used to be—
is dead! The life we have now is the life of Christ. We
now live by a new law called *the law of the Spirit of life
in Christ Jesus.*

Life in the New Law

A person who focuses on keeping rules will experience constant frustration. The purpose of the law is to
show that a right relationship to God is not the result
of conforming to external regulations. Now we live by
this new law which is not based on external demands,
but rather on internal desire. When we understand that
Christ is our life, we are motivated by His desires within us. We *want* to do the things that glorify God. The
law of the Spirit of life in Christ Jesus motivates and
empowers us to live a godly lifestyle. We no longer
focus on rules, but on our relationship to Him. "For
the law of the Spirit of life in Christ Jesus has made me
free from the law of sin and death" (Romans 8:2).

Legalism activates "the law of sin and death"
because the law arouses the desire to sin (Romans 7:5)
and sin leads to death (Romans 6:23). So a person who
takes a legalistic approach to the Christian life can *never*
find victory by trying to keep the law. The certainty of
defeat increases in direct proportion to our effort to live

the Christian life by focusing on rules. The law can tell us what we ought to do, but it can't give us the ability to fulfill its demands. The only thing law can give us is a sense of condemnation over our failure. Second Corinthians 3:7 calls the law "the ministry of death," and verse 9 calls it "the ministry of condemnation." We have died to a system of rules and have been born again into a supernatural relationship of grace! As Watchman Nee explains:

> Grace means that God does something for me; law means that I do something for God. God has certain holy and righteous demands which He places upon me: that is law. Now if law means that God requires something of me for their fulfillment, then deliverance from law means that He no longer requires that from me, but Himself provides it. Law implies that God requires me to do something for Him; deliverance from law implies that He exempts me from doing it, and that in grace He does it Himself. *I need do nothing for God:* that is deliverance from law.[1]

This truth slams hard against the perspective of a legalist. I spent many years of my Christian life trying to do something for God. What a relief to discover that God isn't interested in what we can do for Him. He can do anything that He needs done! He doesn't want what we can do—He just wants us! When Christ is allowed to express His life through us, it will be a ministry of supernatural life, not a religious routine which leaves us frustrated and unfulfilled.

The core of the Christian life doesn't revolve

around *doing*, but is grounded in *being*. The Christian life is the life of Christ. Our focus is a person, not the performance of religious activities. As we experience the law of the Spirit of life in Christ Jesus, godly action is the consequence of His life flowing from us. It is not the result of dedicated effort on our part. *The Amplified Bible* puts it this way:

> Let me ask you this one question: Did you receive the [Holy] Spirit as the result of obeying the Law and doing its works, or was it by hearing [the message of the Gospel] and believing [it]? [Was it from observing a law of rituals or from a message of faith?] Are you so foolish and so senseless and so silly? Having begun [your new life spiritually] with the [Holy] Spirit, are you now reaching perfection [by dependence] on the flesh? (Galatians 3:2-3).

Good question! The only thing we did to enter into the Christian life was to trust Christ. Does God require something different now that we have become Christians? Is it possible that while obeying certain rules had nothing to do with being saved, it becomes very important to God *after* we are saved? Of course not! Then why do so many Christians believe that they must repeatedly rededicate themselves to follow God's rules? It is because Satan knows that the best way to defeat Christians is make them believe that obeying the law is the pathway to victory.

It is impossible for *you* to fulfill the law. If you really want to live a godly lifestyle, the focus of your life must be Him. Not church, not religious activity, not a moral lifestyle, not obeying His commands. Just Him! The only one who can live the Christ-life is Christ. You can rededicate yourself again and again, but at the bottom of it all, you still have *self* trying to live for God. Self-effort is the essence of legalism. It is pointless to pray for God to help you to live for Him. That may be *your* goal, but it isn't *His*. He wants to live His life *through* you.

> By the cross [God] has been cutting us loose from our old natural resources that we might live the life of Another. Of course, from God's standpoint, man has had divine life from the initial moment he was born from above. But just as God revealed the value of the blood to reconcile and forgive, or the value of our union in death with Christ for our deliverance, even so it must come as a revelation that we are cut off from the old source of natural life. Now we are to live and move by the life-resources of Another.[2]

Maybe it seems strange to you that the focus of your life shouldn't be on obedience to God's laws. Yet when you live each day allowing Christ to express Himself as your life, your lifestyle *will* be godly. Jesus didn't break the law when He was here 2,000 years ago. He fulfilled it then, and He will do it again today when you allow Him to live His life through you.

Have you spent your Christian life trying to obey God? How well have you done with your efforts? (If you think you're doing well, you had better reexamine the righteous standard that God requires.) If you have focused on the law as a means to victory, you have experienced considerable frustration in your Christian life. That is exactly what the law is supposed to do to you.

You might be wondering if *anyone* can really live it. Well, Someone can. And He will, when you finally give up your efforts and let Him do it through you.

However, don't think you will passively coast from victory to victory without any battles. When God first revealed the truth of the exchanged life to me, I felt like a new Christian who couldn't imagine ever being tempted to sin again. I lived on such an emotional peak for a while that old thought patterns seemed distant and far removed. But it wasn't long until it became clear that while my old man was dead, the flesh was still very much with me. It was time to come out of the upper room and discover God's way of dealing with those old flesh patterns which had developed over a lifetime.

CHAPTER 7

VICTORY IS
A GIFT

tried everything I could think of to experience victory, but all to no avail. I didn't know that it was by my dying, not doing, that victory was possible. Like all Christians, I had a sincere desire to glorify God. That desire is inherent to the new nature of every believer. At the core of our being, our spirit yearns to express the righteousness of Christ. A Christian whose lifestyle contradicts the holy nature of Christ will inevitably experience anxiety. A sinning Christian is behaving in a way that is unnatural. The spirit is the core of one's being, and at the spirit level the believer was made righteous. So for a Christian to sin is to act against his own nature. Anytime a person behaves unnaturally, he won't feel right about his behavior. There may be a temporary and shallow pleasure in sin, but beneath it all will be a restlessness within the Christian whose lifestyle is sinful. People who do not have the nature of Christ aren't bothered when they sin. They are doing what comes naturally.

Does this mean that Christians will enjoy sinless

perfection? Or course not. Our old nature was put to death with Jesus at the cross, but there is another obstacle to a victorious lifestyle which we must understand. While the old man is dead, the flesh is still an enemy to be reckoned with every day. An earlier chapter defined *the flesh* as "the techniques we use to try to meet our needs, independent of Jesus Christ." The expression of flesh life might be obviously wicked, as evidenced in the life of a person who commits adultery to gratify a sexual or emotional desire. Or the flesh might appear respectable, as in a person who eloquently teaches the Bible in order to gain a sense of significance and affirmation from his ministry. *To walk after the flesh simply means to live a lifestyle which does not rely on Christ as its source.*

All of us have developed flesh patterns. We have learned specific techniques that minimize the risk of painful circumstances in our lives and maximize the opportunity for self-gratification. Until we understand the reality of Christ as our life, our lifestyle will be characterized by these fleshly behavior patterns. One unavoidable result of a flesh-oriented lifestyle is that the spiritual life is always up and down, characterized by inconsistency.

The Flesh and Service

Without a proper understanding of how the flesh operates in our life, our whole perspective on walking in victory will be distorted. For many years my evaluation of my own spiritual life was that I was either "close to God" or "away from the Lord." When I felt defeated I would conclude that I was out of fellowship and needed to get back close to the Lord again. Before I understood that Christ was my life, I was doomed to constant defeat. When I considered myself close to God, I would pour my energy into doing all the things for God that I could do. When I felt I was away from the Lord, I was miserable. Self-condemnation would increase until I finally rededicated myself to Him and started busily doing things for Him again.

I was a manic-depressive Christian! Have you experienced this distorted kind of Christianity? I felt close to God when doing the things I believed that He expected, and far from the Lord when I neglected those responsibilities. However the truth is that God is never closer to us or further from us at any point. If Christ is always in us and we are in Him, how can we ever get closer than that? We may *feel* far from God, but Jesus Christ is always within us, having promised never to leave us.

The victorious Christian life is nothing less than the life of Christ being expressed through the child of God. *Any* behavior which is not dependent on Him living His life through us comes from the flesh. That suggests that it is even possible to be busy doing things *for* God while our actions still stem from the energy of the flesh. *The exchanged life means we depend on His resources, not our own. Flesh life means depending on what I can do.* We may be well respected for our zeal and service to Christ and yet be relying on the flesh. God has no desire to help *us* to live the Christian life or do the work of Christian ministry. He wants to do it Himself—*through* us. Major Ian Thomas has said:

> There is nothing quite so nauseating or pathetic as the flesh trying to be holy! The flesh has a perverted bent for righteousness— but such righteousness as it may achieve is

always self-righteousness; and self-righteousness is always self-conscious righteousness; and self-conscious righteousness is always full of self-praise. This produces the extrovert, who must always be noticed, recognized, consulted, and applauded. On the other hand, when the flesh in pursuit of self-righteousness fails, instead of being filled with self-praise, it is filled with self-pity, and this produces the introvert. A professional "case" for professional counselors![1]

Trying to do something *for* God is a flesh trip! It is possible to be sincere in trying to do something for Him, yet be sincerely wrong. Religious flesh is often a hard pattern for a person to recognize because it is usually applauded by other Christians. Religious service may cause you to be pleased with yourself. Or it may leave you feeling spiritually and emotionally drained. If you find yourself in either place, God may be trying to show you the problem. Many Christians today are exhausted because they understand the Christian life to be primarily a life of service for God. But that isn't true. The Christian life is primarily a life of intimacy *with* God.

There may have been created within you a genuine desire to serve God, out of a sincere sense of gratitude to Christ for dying for you; you may be impelled out of a sense of duty as a Christian, to seek conformity to some pattern of behavior that has been imposed upon you as the norm for Christian living; you may be deeply moved by the need of others around you, and holy ambitions may have been stirred within your heart, to count for God; if, however, all that has happened is that your sins have been forgiven, because you have accepted Christ as the Savior who died for you, leaving you *since* your conversion only with those resources which you had *before* your conversion, then you will have no alternative but to "Christianize" the flesh and try to teach it to "behave" in such a way that it will be godly.

That is a sheer impossibility! The nature of the flesh never changes. No matter how you may coerce it or conform it, it is rotten through and through, even with a Bible under its arm, a check for missions in its hand, and an evangelical look on its face![2]

Any person whose Christian life is centered on service is doomed to a life of frustration. I speak from personal experience. It was a painful realization when God showed me that I was more in love with the ministry than with the One who called me to the ministry. Sooner or later, a person whose life revolves around service will experience burn out. And what a wonderful realization when that day comes—the realization that human energy and efforts *can* burn out, but that the life of Christ will never burn out! Christian service which doesn't overflow from our walk with Christ is nothing but flesh. God cannot receive glory from flesh, regardless of how dedicated it might be.

The Flesh and Sins

A Christian who lives according to the flesh will

often find his spiritual experience to be high voltage some of the time and a drained battery at other times. Such a person is always on the lookout for anything that will give another "spiritual charge." I have read books, been to conferences and seminars, attended revival meetings, listened to tapes, and done a hundred other things in an effort to "get my battery charged" for Jesus. It was discouraging that life always drained my battery faster than I could keep it recharged. Have you experienced that problem? When my "spiritual battery" was weak, I found myself vulnerable to sinful flesh patterns. When I sinned I would sooner or later feel guilty and ask the Lord to help me to live for Him. I resolved to do whatever it took to keep myself charged.

However a Christian doesn't experience victory over sins by keeping himself charged up for Jesus. Christ Himself *is* our power over sin. As we allow Him to express His life through us, we will experience continuous victory over temptation. It is important to make this distinction: Christ does not *give* us the victory; instead, He *is* our victory! Consider these promises from God concerning the source of victorious Christian living:

• *"But thanks be to God, who gives us the victory through our Lord Jesus Christ"* (1 Corinthians 15:57). The Bible clearly says here that victory is a *gift* that comes through Jesus Christ. So if we have the Lord Jesus Christ, victory is ours.

• *"Now thanks be to God who always leads us in triumph in Christ, and through us diffuses the fragrance of His knowledge in every place"* (2 Corinthians 2:14). How

VICTORY IS A GIFT • 97

often does God lead us in triumph? Always! What is
the source of the triumph we may experience daily?
Christ!

• *"Yet in all these things we are more than conquerors
through Him who loved us"* (Romans 8:37). Life will get
tough at times (verses 35-36), but we aren't just conquerors—we are *more* than conquerors *through Him!*

Do you get the picture? We don't experience victory by fighting, instead we enjoy it by faith! As we
abide in Christ and allow Him to live His life through
us, we live in victory. *"And this is the victory that has
overcome the world—our faith"* (1 John 5:4). Why would
Christians want to get their spiritual batteries charged,
when we have an omnipotent "power plant" within us
that can continuously be activated by faith in Him?

Focusing on Him, Not on Sin!

A guaranteed way to be defeated by the flesh is to
focus on the sins that we want to avoid. That's like
going on a diet and then reading the menu at Pizza Hut
every day just so we'll know the foods we want to
avoid! We don't experience victory over the flesh by
being preoccupied with it. We are to be obsessed with
Jesus, not sin. "For those who live according to the
flesh set their minds on the things of the flesh, but
those who live according to the Spirit, the things of the
Spirit. For to be carnally minded is death, but to be
spiritually minded is life and peace" (Romans 8:5-6).

Philip had been involved in adultery several times
over the past few years. He had come from a home
where his own parents had what has been called
"an open marriage." They both often brought other

partners into the home. What would happen during those times was no secret. Neither of his parents expressed their love for him. The only affection he had seen them give to anyone was toward those with whom they had affairs. Philip's own low self-esteem, coupled together with the absence of a proper role model for marriage, influenced his adulterous lifestyle. He had received Christ and wanted to be faithful to his wife, but he was afraid. For many years he had been programmed for erotic behavior. "I am scared that I'm going to fall back into that life again," he expressed one day. "I don't want to, but everywhere I turn, the temptation is in front of me." In an effort to keep from failing, Philip had given away his television because of all the sexual stimuli on the screen. He was apprehensive about going to any movies, for fear that what he saw might put him in the wrong frame of mind. "I can't even look at some of the billboards as I drive to work each morning," he complained. He felt that he was walking through a minefield where he might accidently step into a temptation and suddenly see his Christianity be blown apart.

Philip's outlook is not uncommon, but he was giving more credit to the enemy than he deserves. Satan can't *make* a Christian sin. But an attitude like Philip's will lead to sin if it isn't adjusted to God's truth. The Bible says that God is able "to keep you from stumbling" (Jude 24). His problem wasn't that he was spiritually weak; the omnipotent power of Almighty God is in him. His problem was that he focused on the temptation to sin and not on Christ. He confessed greater confidence in Satan's ability to cause him to fall than in the ability of the Holy Spirit to keep him from falling.

God's purpose is that the focus of our whole life be on Him. Our minds are to be set continuously on the Spirit of Christ. When our minds are fixed on Jesus, we will experience a quality of life characterized by the peace of God. But preoccupation with sin stimulates internal conflict that will ultimately enslave us to the very sins we are trying to avoid.

"Walk in the Spirit, and you shall not fulfill the lust of the flesh" (Galatians 5:16). The key to overcoming the flesh is walking in the Spirit. There has been much discussion among Christians about the Spirit-filled walk. The heart of walking in the Spirit is allowing the Spirit of Christ to do the walking through us. That is God's prescribed order. We often reverse the order and try to overcome the sinful desires of the flesh, so that we might be able to walk in the Spirit. However, we can't clean up our act to become spiritual. It isn't possible to do things backwards from what God says and also experience success!

It is the life of Christ within us that gives us the victory. Just as His death and resurrection delivered us from the penalty of sin, so His life frees us from sin's power as we faithfully abide in Him. "For if when we were enemies we were reconciled to God through the death of His Son, much more, having been reconciled, we shall be saved *by His life*" (Romans 5:10, emphasis mine).

Does it make sense that Jesus would *die* for our sin and then not provide a way for victory over sins after we are saved? We are saved from sin's power *by His life* as it is expressed through us. I'll never think of getting my spiritual battery charged again. When we abide in Christ, it is like turning a switch into the "on" position and allowing the full power of Jesus Christ to flow through us. When we choose to rest in His life, we experience victory. When we choose not to abide, we flip the switch to the "off" position and we fail.

Christ's life is the remedy for every temptation. It's the answer to Philip's vulnerability toward adultery. The life of Christ being expressed through him each day will save him from an adulterous lifestyle. He simply needs to choose to abide in Christ each moment. As long as he does that, Christ will effectively handle any temptation that may come along.

Flesh Will Always Be Flesh

For some time after God revealed the truth of the exchanged life to me, I lived on an emotional mountaintop. Then the time came when my flesh reared its head again. I'm sorry to say that my flesh hasn't improved—it's just as ugly as it ever was. But please understand that it looks ugly only when I see it through the eyes of Christ. At times when I fail to abide in Him, it actually looks appealing. Let's face it: if temptation has no appeal, what's the big deal about being tempted? Yes, sometimes those flesh patterns do look enticing and I still yield to the flesh. There, I've said it. But don't be too quick to judge me—your flesh is no better than mine. Flesh won't improve through Christian maturity, spiritual warfare, or anything else. The only remedy for flesh is walking in the Spirit. I have found that when I rest in Christ's sufficiency, I experience victory; and when I don't, I experience defeat. It's that simple.

When Christians fail to abide in Christ, they assert their own independence. Sin came into the world when Adam and Eve chose to assert their independence from God by their disobedience. Christians who are not abiding in Him are walking in a state of continuous sin, regardless of their actions. This *attitude of independence* will eventually give birth to specific *sins*, which are the fruit of abiding in self. For that reason, it should come as no surprise that Christians sin when they don't abide in Christ. What else could possibly happen?

If I tell you that a man jumped off a ten-story building, would it occur to you to ask, "Did he fall?" That question would be ridiculous. Any man who jumps off a building will fall because of the consistency of the law of gravity. The only way he wouldn't fall is if a greater law took effect. For instance, if he were in a hang glider he wouldn't fall because the law of aerodynamics would supersede the law of gravity in that case. The law of gravity is not suspended, but it is overcome by a greater law. Flesh will always respond to the law of sin and death. But abiding in Christ causes us to experience the law of the Spirit of life in Christ Jesus, enabling us to soar above the temptations of the flesh.

We can take no credit when we triumph over the flesh, since the victory has been *given* to us by God. Could the Children of Israel take credit for the victory at Jericho when God knocked the walls flat? The only thing they did was to believe what God said about how He was going to give them the victory. They marched around the wall just as God told them to, in spite of the fact that their actions contradicted human logic. At the prescribed time, they shouted in victory, the wall fell flat, and God gave them the city. What would have happened if they had chosen their own battle plan instead of obeying the Lord? They would have been defeated, regardless of the ingenuity of their plan and the strength of their army.

We experience victory in the Christian life as we

receive God's gift in faith. It might seem logical that victory would come by a fight, but fighting for victory is the surest way to experience defeat. God has determined to *give* it to those who will receive it by faith in His Son. As Charles Trumbull says:

> The great truth that so many earnest, surrendered Christians have even yet failed to see is that salvation is a twofold gift; freedom from the *penalty* of sin, and freedom from the *power* of sin. All Christians have received in Christ as their Savior their freedom from the penalty of their sins, and they have received this as an outright gift from God. But many Christians have not yet realized that they may, in the same way, and by the same kind of faith in the same God and Savior, receive now and here the freedom from the power of their sins which was won for them by their Savior on the cross and in His resurrection victory. Even though they know clearly that their own efforts have nothing to do with their salvation from the *penalty* of their sins, they are yet deceived by the Adversary into believing that somehow their own efforts must play a part in their present victory over the *power* of their sins. *Our efforts can not only never play any part in our victory over the power of sin, but they can and do effectually prevent such victory.* . . . We are to use our will to accept the gift of victory; we are not to make an effort to win the victory.[3]

At times I experience a struggle against the law of

sin and death within me. Because of an understanding of *truth*, I have learned to recognize that struggle as a red flag. God doesn't intend for us to struggle for the victory. As we rest in Him, we enjoy the victory of His life. It is impossible to struggle and rest at the same time!

CHAPTER 8

THE VICE
OF VALUES

I really began to enjoy life when I gave up my Christian values. For many years my life was built around those principles which I believed embodied the essence of the Christian life. I thought it was a noble cause to boldly defend those values. I lamented the fact that our country had abandoned its Judeo-Christian ethic.

But discovering how to walk in grace has totally reshaped my perspective. I now recognize that no value system, Christian or otherwise, can express the essence of Christianity. A life built on Christian values is a caricature of New Testament Christianity. It is not God's purpose that our lives be built on a *system of values*. It is His desire that they be built on the *person* of His Son. Value systems may influence behavior, but God is not interested in systems of living. He is interested in relationships. An intimate relationship with Him will produce a godly lifestyle. A focus on behavior will not create intimacy with God or a godly lifestyle.

Two Trees in the Garden of Eden

The idea of building a lifestyle around a system of right and wrong dates back to the dawn of mankind. God's purpose in creating people was that He might enjoy them, expressing His loving nature to them and through them. He lovingly placed Adam and Eve in the Garden of Eden and gave them reign over the garden and all that was in it. One aspect of freedom is choice, for where there is no choice there is no real freedom. Consequently, two trees were placed in the Garden about which Adam and Even would make a choice. How they chose would determine not only their own destiny, but the destiny of all future generations. "And out of the ground the LORD God made every tree grow that is pleasant to the sight and good for food. The tree of life was also in the midst of the garden and the tree of the knowledge of good and evil" (Genesis 2:9).

• *The Tree of Life.* The tree of life is a picture of the Lord Jesus. A basic principle of biblical interpretation is that the Old Testament is understood in light of New Testament revelation. The New Testament affirms repeatedly that Jesus is Life. The reason a person possesses eternal life when he is a Christian is that Christ lives within him. To receive Him is to receive Life! Jesus said that He came so that we might have life (John 10:10). As we abide in Him, His life flows out of us like rivers of living water. It isn't that we struggle to produce a flow of Divine Life. His life just naturally flows out of Christians who are abiding in Him. God intended that Adam and Eve should live by His life all their days. As long as He was the only source they had in this world, questions of right and wrong would have never arisen. Eating from the second tree is where the trouble for mankind began.

• *The Tree of the Knowledge of Good and Evil.* God placed a multitude of trees in the Garden. There was only one tree from which Adam and Eve were forbidden to eat. It was the tree of the knowledge of good and evil. The prohibition was for their own good. Remember that God created this tree and gave them a choice, because without choice there could be no freedom. God wanted them to *choose* Him. That choice would provide eternal life. Adam and Eve were told that in the day they ate from the tree of the knowledge of good and evil, they would die. So the choice was clear—life or death. They could continue to live in total dependence on God or choose independence from Him. Satan convinced Eve that God was withholding something good from them and she ate from the forbidden tree. Adam did the same, and suddenly their eyes were opened. For the first time they became conscious of good and evil. From that day forward, every deed of their life would be judged by a value system of right and wrong. However, that was not God's original plan. His desire was that they simply allow Him to be the source and authority of their life.

Back to the 1990s

Now let's jump back into the twentieth century. As a result of Adam and Eve's sin, their descendants today still live by the choice they made. Every society defines right and wrong according to its own standards, and people's lives are judged on the basis of conformity to those standards. Yet God's purpose for mankind hasn't changed from His design in the Garden of Eden. He still wants us to find our source in His life, not in laws dictating right and wrong.

When we become Christians, we possess the divine life of Jesus Christ. As we abide in Christ, His life flows out of us producing a righteous lifestyle. Before I understood that Christ is my life, my whole lifestyle was characterized by an obsession with right and wrong. Yet, if one is not abiding in Christ, every action is wrong. To abide in Him is to walk in faith; to fail to abide in Christ is to walk after the flesh. Anytime we do things on our own, it is sin, regardless of how our actions may appear. This is exactly what Paul meant when he said, "Whatever is not from faith is sin" (Romans 14:23). When we fail to abide in Christ, sin is not the root of the problem, but the symptoms. The real issue is that we are living out of our own sufficiency, independently of Christ.

Contemporary Christians are involved in endless debates over questions of right and wrong. Is it wrong for a Christian to drink wine? How about a daiquiri? Can a Christian listen to the rock group Guns 'n Roses? How about country singer Garth Brooks? Should a Christian attend R-rated movies? How about PG movies with bad language? The list is never-ending. When we realize that our lifestyle should express the life of Christ within us, we realize that we have been asking all the wrong questions!

Even good behavior which isn't an expression of Christ within us is a sin. Remember that the tree was of good *and* evil. Christians are quick to acknowledge that deeds of human goodness demonstrated by one who isn't a Christian mean nothing to God. Romans 8:8 says that "those who are in the flesh cannot please God." Why? Because they are living out of their own resources, not by faith in Christ. "Without faith it is impossible to please Him" (Hebrews 11:6). God isn't impressed by human goodness because it is nothing more than self-righteousness. Even when a Christian lives from his own resources, his good deeds are nothing more than self-righteous behavior. Do you see the problem? The fruit comes from the wrong tree.

Ask the Right Question

The definitive question in the life of the believer is not, "Would it be wrong for me to do this?" but, "Am I abiding in Christ at this moment?" An unsaved person evaluates behavior on the basis of right and wrong, but the lifestyle of a Christian is to flow from the activity of Christ. If the lifestyle of a Christian is built around a value system, there is little difference between that and the lifestyle of an unbeliever. Many unbelievers express a desire to live according to the values embodied in the Golden Rule or the Ten Commandments.

Recently I saw a billboard with the Ten Commandments printed on it. Beneath them it read: "The Ten Commandments—God's way to save America!" That may sound good, but it's wrong. The Ten Commandments outline a moral code which reflect the righteous nature of a holy God. However, the only thing that the Ten Commandments can do to America is minister condemnation and death to our nation. The purpose of law is to establish an awareness of need. It can diagnose the spiritual disease, but it offers absolutely no hope for a cure. The billboard would have been correct had it read, "Jesus Christ—God's way to save America." To try to impose righteousness on a nation by incorporating values based on law, even the Ten Commandments, is futile. Apart from Christ, can any nation observe God's commandments? What power would people possess to enable them to obey God's laws apart from Christ? The answer for a perishing society is not values. The answer is Christ. Is this true only for unsaved people? Does it make sense that unbelievers can't be saved by values yet for Christians values suddenly take on great importance?

Why You Should Give Up Your Values!

I highly recommend that you give up your Christian values. You may find this statement startling, but I want to shake you into serious thought. I'm not advocating moral anarchy. Nor am I suggesting that how you live is unimportant. What I *am* saying is that focusing on a value system is not God's intended way for you to live. God never proposed your lifestyle to be built around the principle of right and wrong. To do so is damaging in several ways.

• *An obsession with right and wrong makes people self-conscious instead of God-conscious.* Before the Fall, good and evil were irrelevant to Adam and Eve. Their focus was not to be on their own behavior; instead, they were to build their life around their relationship with God. Focusing on behavior would make them self-conscious; God's purpose was that they focus on Him. After the Fall, they suddenly became aware of their own identity separate from God. Until that time they had been God-conscious to such an extent that they were unaware of their own nakedness. In a manner of speaking, they hadn't even looked at themselves. When they ate from the tree of the knowledge of good and evil, they became egocentric. They began to evaluate their own appearance, actions, and attitudes. Their eyes were off God and on themselves.

That's what concentrating on good and evil will do to you. Until I came to understand the grace walk, I spent considerable time and energy in self-analysis. I classified every word, thought, and deed as right or wrong. When I found myself making more entries in the "wrong" column, I began to feel guilty, and nothing robs a person of joy in his Christian life like guilt. Now I don't measure my life by right and wrong. My aim is simply to abide in Christ. By doing that, issues of right and wrong become incidental. As I abide in Christ, His attitude and actions are expressed through me. When I fail to abide in Him, my actions would have no godly value, even if they were a mix of Billy Graham and Mother Teresa!

Do you find yourself absorbed with self-analysis? Vance Havner spoke of people who

> . . . spend their days in a perpetual clinic, with themselves as both doctor and patient. The devil has a lot of fun with sensitive, conscientious souls given to introspection. He makes them connoisseurs of moods, specialists in self-examination, and much given to examining their sincerity. They worry because they do not pray enough, read the Bible enough, testify enough, rejoice enough. But very often people who are so troubled will not find relief by increasing their performance and stepping up the quantity of prayers turned out or chapters read. Very likely they will be whipping up jaded nerves already exhausted, and will merely increase their load.[1]

Richard had spent two weeks in the hospital because of depression. As I visited with him, we had only spoken for a few minutes when he began to express his anxiety. "I prayed to receive Christ when I was twenty-nine," he explained. "I was sincere at the time, but lately I've wondered if I'm really a Christian. Maybe I didn't really mean it." As we talked for the next hour, he poured out his doubts. Not only did he question his sincerity at the time he confessed faith in Christ, but he even wondered aloud if he had *said* the right thing when he prayed. He was worried about whether he had actually repented. It was obvious that he had dissected his salvation experience piece by piece, examining every thought and word. He was paralyzed with fear that he might not be a Christian because he hadn't done the right things in the right way. The anxiety he experienced about his relationship to God had carried over into every relationship. He meticulously scrutinized every detail of his life and this drove him deeper and deeper into depression.

Richard's experience isn't that uncommon. While few find themselves hospitalized because of obsessive introspection, many people are spiritually frustrated as a result of constant self-examination. No Christian whose focus is on *self* is free to enjoy life. Do you find yourself constantly grading your spiritual life to make sure you are still passing the tests you give yourself? Take your eyes off yourself and place your full attention on Christ! As you move from a performance-based lifestyle to the grace walk, you will find it isn't necessary to be obsessed with your own attitudes and actions. The Holy Spirit within you will call your attention to anything that needs to be changed. Then, as you yield those areas of your life to Him, He will change them for you. Your responsibility is simply to rest in Christ. He will do whatever needs to be done. Now *that* is grace!

• *An obsession with right and wrong emphasizes human values instead of godly virtues.* Values are the structure of a belief system, and it is on this structure that a person builds a lifestyle. That's why legalists emphasize having the right values. They argue that wrong values lead to a wrong lifestyle. Their logic can't be disputed. Immoral values certainly won't produce a moral lifestyle. Morality stems from honorable values. However this approach doesn't require divine life because it is *behavior-oriented.* Unsaved persons can adopt moral values, even those of the Christian community. They can build their lives around principles of human goodness and perhaps be fairly successful at it.

But the believers shouldn't build their lifestyle around any thing. They aren't involved in a building project. Their goal is not to have a moral lifestyle but a *miraculous* one! They are to rest in Christ and allow Him to express His life through them. As they abide in Christ, the divine virtues of Jesus will be revealed through their attitudes and actions.

Can you see how the desire to live right is an improper goal for the Christian? Unsaved people often want that much. Doing right things can be the result of living within a right value system, but living *righteously* is the outcome of Christ expressing His divine virtues through us. It's a feeble goal for a Christian to only want to live correctly. A person with the divine nature of Christ within is capable of much more than that!

Do you understand how human values can hinder

you from experiencing the expression of Christ's life through you? When my son Andrew was about five years old, I took him to buy a pair of shoes. He tried on a pair of dress shoes he liked. I felt the shoe and knew there was plenty of room between his toe and the end of the shoe. "How does the shoe feel on your foot?" I asked.

"It feels good," he replied. With his assurance that this was the pair of shoes he wanted, we bought them and went home.

About three days later he complained that his shoes hurt his feet. Melanie knelt to check the fit and found his toes pushing against the toe of the shoe. "Steve, these shoes are too small!" she said to me in that "I knew I should have done it myself" tone of voice that wives sometimes have.

"I felt his foot and it felt all right to me," I answered. Turning to Andrew, I said, "Son, I thought you told me that the shoes felt good."

He answered, "They do if I keep my toes turned under."

That's how values fit the Christian. They feel pretty good "if you keep your toes turned under." As a legalist, I emphasized the importance of values. I determined to find the Christian size and wear them, but they never felt quite right. Since I have discovered grace, I realize how uncomfortable I really was all those years. Do you sense an uncomfortable fit, no matter how hard you try to live by your Christian values? Kick off your shoes and run barefoot through the fields of His grace! He will make sure that you don't step in the wrong places.

- *An obsession with right and wrong stresses law*

instead of life. The criterion of right and wrong is grounded in the law of God. It is through the law that a person understands the difference between right and wrong. The apostle Paul said that he would never have known what was wrong without the instruction of the law. "I would not have known sin except through the law. For I would not have known covetousness unless the law had said, 'You shall not covet'" (Romans 7:7).

Without the law a person has no gauge for right and wrong. The principle of right and wrong is inseparably linked to God's laws. They *cannot* be separated. Paul goes so far as to say that "apart from the law sin was dead" (Romans 7:8). Right and wrong have no life, no meaning, apart from the law.

It is impossible to judge what is right and wrong without the law. The law is a codified expression of God's righteousness, an external picture of God's eternal purity. The law says to those who see it, "This is how you are supposed to look." It shows us that we don't look right, but it can't help us change the way we look.

People whose lives are built around an obsession with right and wrong will forever be frustrated. They look at the law and see what they should and shouldn't do. Yet they can never effect the changes that the law reveals are necessary. Paul referred to himself as a "wretched" man, literally, a miserable man, when he tried to live under the law. But remember the good news we discussed in chapter 6? We aren't required to live under the law anymore. "But now we have been delivered from the law, having died to what we were held by, so that we should serve in the newness of the Spirit and not in the oldness of the letter" (Romans 7:6).

Because we have been crucified with Christ, we have been delivered from the law. We are no longer required to live under a system of rules which outline right and wrong behavior. We are now free to enjoy life in the Spirit. God promised the Old Testament saints that a day would come when He would write His law on the hearts of His people. That day has come!

You were married to the law before you were a Christian. But when you died with Christ, the marriage was dissolved. Then you were born a second time. In this new life you have a different husband. It's Mr. Grace, Himself—Jesus! Mr. Law was a demanding husband who was never satisfied, regardless of how many right things you did. He didn't just claim to be perfect; he actually was perfect and he demanded the same from you. He wouldn't help you do anything right, but was quick to point out when you did wrong. Mr. Grace is very different. Whatever He wants done, He just does Himself. Any burden He asks you to carry is light. In fact, whenever He asks you to pick up a burden and carry it, He carries you! He's such a gracious Husband. You might say He is always "full of grace and truth."

For many years I assumed that Mr. Grace was the same kind of husband to me as Mr. Law had been. One day He said to me, "I'm not Mr. Law! Will you stop expecting me to act like he did? You aren't married to him anymore." Although I had been married to Mr. Grace for a long time, it was the first time I *really* heard what He was saying. He doesn't condemn me. He loves me just as I am! He sees my faults and gently works in my life to cause me to grow, but never gets disgusted with me. Divorce from Him is impossible. I am one with Him "until death do us part," and neither of us is ever going to die!

Any marriage is difficult when the bride has to walk on eggshells to keep from making her husband angry. Has your Christian life revolved around evaluating your actions and attitudes on the basis of right and wrong? If so, you are still living under law. How can you enjoy your relationship to Jesus if you are always checking the rules to find out what you can and can't do? He doesn't care about rules. Right and wrong are incidental to Him. He loves you and wants you to enjoy His love and then love Him right back! That's what marriage is all about. Mr. Law is still alive, but you'll never again be married to him. The new you will be one with Christ for eternity.

A Christian beginning the grace walk may be tempted to project the personality of Mr. Law onto Jesus, and that's a tragic mistake. As I began living my Christian life under grace, I wondered if I should be careful not to get out of balance with grace. I questioned whether or not pure grace might encourage me to sin. But I soon learned that one single aspect of my newfound freedom would do more to motivate me to live a godly lifestyle than a thousand laws could ever do. In fact, it's the *only* thing that will keep a Christian from sinning.

CHAPTER 9

ALL YOU NEED IS LOVE

ho does she think I do all this for?" Lance asked with obvious irritation. He and his wife, Brenda, were in my office for marriage counseling. For the past fifteen minutes, with tears streaming down her cheeks, she had told me how he failed to meet her emotional needs. Lance was a successful businessman in town. In fact, he was one of the most wealthy men I knew.

"Lance, you stay gone from home all the time and even when you're home, you *aren't* home," Brenda continued.

"She didn't complain when I took her to Europe last year," he said, looking at me as if asking for my understanding. "I don't hear her complain about the jewelry I've bought her or the lake house we enjoy *together*."

"You just don't get it!" Brenda blurted out with louder volume. "I want what we used to have. I didn't have the *things* we do now, but I had *you*. What you say you're doing for me doesn't mean a thing to me when I don't feel that you love me."

Lance's impasse with his wife reflects the problem that prevented me from enjoying conscious intimacy with God. He was focused on doing things *for* Brenda, while what she really wanted was intimacy *with* him. There have been times in my life when I was so busy trying to do things *for* God that I lost all sense of intimacy *with* Him. However, as a Christian moves from a legalistic, performance-based lifestyle into the grace walk, he will find an increasing interest in developing intimacy with Christ. Whereas there might have been a sense of fulfillment in *activity* before, the person coming to understand Christ as life will be consumed with knowing Him above everything else.

Now that I am learning to walk in grace, I have come to *delight* in my relationship with God. Have you ever heard someone say, "I love this person, but I'm not *in love* with him"? That best describes the change I have seen take place as I have appropriated the exchanged life. I loved the Lord while trying to do the things for Him that I thought would please Him. After He revealed Himself to me as my life, I have found myself becoming more and more *in love* with Him. Being in love with Jesus has made all the difference in my relationship to Him. I now *enjoy* the relationship in a new way. Do you enjoy your relationship to Christ? Do you find pleasure in intimacy with Him? That's what He wants more than anything. He is the groom and we are the bride. Every groom finds his greatest joy in knowing that his wife experiences ecstatic joy in her intimacy with him.

Have you ever seen two newlyweds together? They are lavish in their expressions of love for each other. The Bible tells a love story that illustrates the kind of intimacy that Christ wants to have with those who are His.

The Song of Solomon is a romantic story about the intimacy between King Solomon and a young Shulamite girl. The intimacy between these two is syrupy sweet. As the story begins, the first words she speaks are, "Let him kiss me with the kisses of his mouth, for your love is better than wine" (1:2). Then she expresses how much she wants him. She is hungry for his love. One night the Shulamite girl lies down to sleep, but she can't rest because she wants to be with him.

> By night on my bed I sought the one I love; I sought him, but I did not find him. "I will arise now," I said, "and go about the city; in the streets and in the squares I will seek the one I love." I sought him, but I did not find him. The watchmen who go about the city found me; I said, "Have you seen the one I love?" Scarcely had I passed by them, when I found the one I love. I held him and would not let him go, until I had brought him to the house of my mother and into the chamber of her who conceived me (3:1-4).

Wouldn't you agree that this is the kind of bride every man wants when he gets married? She was consumed with him. Her love and desire for him was the driving force in her actions. No risk or sacrifice was too great as she sought intimacy with him. If necessary, she would go out into the city streets in the middle of the night to find him. That's how much she wanted him.

Do you realize that God wants us to desire Him like that? How foolish I was when I thought that God's main interest was in what I did for Him. I lived as if He wanted a maid to serve Him, when what He really wants is a bride who loves Him so much that she is consumed with knowing Him intimately!

Not only did the bride want her husband, but he wanted her even more. He was the one who initiated the love relationship in the beginning. He savored every small expression of love she gave to him. He said to her:

> You have ravished my heart, my sister, my spouse; you have ravished my heart with one look of your eyes, with one link of your neck- lace. How fair is your love, my sister, my spouse! How much better than wine is your love, and the scent of your perfumes than all spices. Your lips, O my spouse, drip as the honeycomb; honey and milk are under your tongue; and the fragrance of your garments is like the fragrance of Lebanon (4:9-11).

Do you sense the kind of relationship these two enjoyed? The Song of Solomon is so candid that some have questioned why it is in the Bible. The Holy Spirit gave us this story to show us the kind of intimate rela- tionship that Christ wants with His bride.

Jesus Wants More Than "I Surrender All"

I grew up in church singing, "I Surrender All." It's a good song which stresses the importance of giving every- thing to Jesus. It could be understood in light of the kind of absolute surrender I experienced when I lay crying on the floor behind my desk. However, as we progress into the grace walk we must move beyond surrender. Even as a legalist I stressed the importance of surrendering every- thing to God; yet, we are Christ's bride, not His hostage. I'm not suggesting that it isn't important to surrender ourselves totally to God, but He wants more than that. Nobody wants a frigid bride. Every groom wants his bride to eagerly desire him, not just "surrender all" to him. As you move into a fuller understanding of grace, intimacy with the Lord Jesus will become the consuming passion of your life. However, it may be necessary to work through some faulty beliefs before you can *feel* intimate with Him.

The Bible uses human relationships to illustrate how we are to relate to God. The Song of Solomon compares our relationship to Christ with that of a husband and wife who are madly in love with each other. Another story that exemplifies the love between God and His children is the parable of the Prodigal Son. This is a story about intimacy, and the wayward son's attitude about his relationship to his father might reflect some barriers in your life which have hindered real intimacy with God.

• *He believed he was not accepted by his father.* When he ran out of resources and determined to return to his father, he rehearsed the speech he intended to use to gain acceptance when he returned home. "Father, I have sinned against heaven and before you, and I am no longer worthy to be called your son. Make me like one of your hired servants" (Luke 15:18-19).

I used to believe that this parable was a lesson on forgiveness; but studying it from a grace perspective makes its meaning clear. It's not about forgiveness but about *acceptance*. Here is a young rebel who thought he was unworthy of his father's acceptance because of his sinful behavior. He determined to go home and ask his father's forgiveness. His sense of unworthiness caused him to believe that he could only hope to be a servant. Yet the story clearly demonstrates that the father had *already* forgiven him and was ready to fully accept him when he returned home. In fact, when his father saw him in the distance, he ran toward him and fell on his neck, kissing him. The son then tried to give his prepared speech.

> But the father said to his servants, "Bring out the best robe and put it on him, and put a ring on his hand and sandals on his feet. And bring the fatted calf here and kill it, and let us eat and be merry; for this my son was dead and is alive again; he was lost and is found." And they began to be merry (verses 22-23).

We hear much about the importance of asking for God's forgiveness when we sin. Yet the Bible clearly teaches that total forgiveness was given to us when we received Christ. God has forgiven us of our *sin nature*. That means that every individual sin we would commit was forgiven.

After I had preached on the subject of forgiveness one day, Denise came to me. "Steve, are you saying that even my *future* sins are already forgiven?"

"Denise, when did Jesus pay the penalty for your sins?" I asked.

"Two thousand years ago, on the cross," she answered.

"How many of your sins were future at that time?"

An expression of recognition came on her face. She smiled and answered, "All of them!"

God didn't deposit forgiveness into an account with our name on it so that we can make forgiveness withdrawals when we need it. When we were born again, He emptied the entire forgiveness account on us! Our debt was paid in full when Christ died, and it became effective in our lives when we turned to Him in faith. Was the prodigal son's father angry with him at any time? There is absolutely no hint of that in the Scripture. He just wanted his son to see the foolishness of his behavior and come on home. The father never stopped accepting the son, although the prodigal felt that way.

If Satan can cause you to feel that God doesn't accept you because of bad behavior, he can keep you in the far country for a longer time. However, when you know that your Father loves and fully accepts you at all times, you feel an inward motivation to see the foolishness of your sins and to come running home, back into His arms.

Is there a place for confession in the Christian's life? Yes, if confession means acknowledging the foolishness of disobedience to the Father and then praising Him that we are *already* forgiven and accepted by Him. We don't need to beg for forgiveness. The Father relates to us from a forgiving heart because He loves us unconditionally. Do you *feel* unaccepted by God? If so, your feelings are telling you a lie! In Christ you are totally accepted by God! It's hard to passionately love someone you believe doesn't accept you. Failure to understand God's acceptance will create a barrier to intimacy.

• *He didn't understand his identity.* Because the prodigal didn't understand his own identity, he believed he was unworthy of an intimate relationship with his father. He thought that he had forfeited the right to relate to his father as a son and that his father would reject him. He saw himself as a bad person who could only hope to be a servant in his father's house. His attitude is common among Christians today.

Many who know that they have been forgiven still see themselves as bad people who need to prove to God how sorry they are for their sins by working hard for Him. Before entering the grace walk, I asked God to forgive my sins many times and promised Him that I would read the Bible more diligently, pray more consistently, witness more fervently. I didn't think that I actually had to earn His forgiveness, but I did feel compelled to prove my sincerity. I thought that it would please Him if I renewed my commitment to *do* things that I believed He wanted me to do. My prayers were often characterized by my groveling before God, promising to do better next time.

Was it necessary for the prodigal to grovel? Did the father show any reluctance to receive him? This boy was his son! Nothing would ever change that. He was his son *before* he went to the far country, while he was in the far country, and when he came *back* from the far country. Nothing changes sonship. The prodigal had forgotten who he was, but the father had never forgotten for a moment.

It is important to realize that the father had *given* him his inheritance. Do you think he suspected how the son would waste it? He had lived with his boy every day and knew his weaknesses. It didn't shock him when the son left home for the far country. He allowed him to leave, knowing that he would probably waste the money on a wild fling. Do you think your sins surprise God? *He knows you.* Nothing you do surprises an omniscient God.

It often troubled me when I thought I had disappointed God, but really that's not possible. Disappointment is the result of an unfulfilled expectation. God isn't capable of disappointment, since He already knows how we will respond in every situation. I'm not implying that God doesn't care when we sin. It grieves the heart of our loving Father when He sees us make foolish choices, but it doesn't surprise Him.

Why did the prodigal's father allow him to leave, knowing what he would do in the far country? Grace! Is a Christian free to do whatever he wants to do? Yes. Your Heavenly Father will allow you to go to the far country if you choose. As Paul said, "All things are lawful for me, but all things are not helpful" (1 Corinthians 6:12).

In the last chapter, we said that believers aren't under the laws of right and wrong anymore. We are free to sin, but when we have a proper understanding of our identity, we will realize that while something may be lawful, it isn't necessarily helpful. In fact, it may be harmful. Does saying that "all things are lawful" suggest that sin is okay in God's eyes? No! Living under grace means that we *can* sin if we so choose. We are free to make foolish choices.

If you are just beginning to seriously contemplate the difference between walking in legalism and under grace, you probably are asking the question, "Is he saying that since grace covers *all* sins, I can go out and sin if that's what I want to do?" Yes, that's exactly what I'm saying. However, before you throw the book down, finish this paragraph. You see, the question about being able to go right on in sin since grace covers it all is not new. When Paul preached grace, people asked the same question. Romans 5 is about how we are dead to laws regulating right and wrong.

Then Paul begins Romans 6 asking the question he knew would be on everybody's mind. "What shall we say then? Shall we continue in sin that grace may abound?" He knew they would be asking that question, just as people do today whenever pure grace is taught. He answers the question by reminding them that they *died* to sin.

Yes, you *can* sin. However when you understand your identity in Christ, you don't *want* to sin. Understanding your identity produces a desire for intimate fellowship with your Heavenly Father. If you don't know who you are, you may see yourself as a servant who must make restitution for sin. Servants find it difficult to enjoy an intimate love relationship with their masters. However, sons and fathers are able to enjoy each other. Do you see yourself primarily as God's child or as His servant?

A Christian who doesn't believe he is totally accepted by God, or who doesn't understand his identity, finds it hard to be intimate with God. Intimacy develops between those who share themselves with each other. This can happen between the Christian and God only as the believer comes to a biblical understanding of his relationship to the Heavenly Father.

Love and New Testament Commandments

The only genuine motivation in the Christian life that will consistently sustain a godly lifestyle is love. Any other motivation will eventually fail. If contemporary Christians spent as much time developing loving intimacy with Christ as is spent in defining proper Christian behavior, the world would be a different place. It isn't without basis that the unsaved world sees Christianity as a religion with a particular system of behavior. Many Christians make that their focus too. They want to know God's commandments in every area of life so they can keep them.

What place do the commandments of the New Testament have in the life of a believer? Does being free from
the law mean that we don't need to obey the biblical
commands? There are two ways to view the commands
of the New Testament. One is law-oriented; the other is
from the perspective of love which understands grace.

A Christian who views the commandments of the
New Testament from the standpoint of law sees them
in a negative way. To him, the commands are something that he *ought* to do. They hang heavy over him,
constantly reminding him of all the things he *must* do
to be fully obedient to God. In the life of a legalist,
they invoke a compelling sense of *need*. He feels that
he should *try* to obey them, because that is what God
expects.

Mark came to me one day with his spiritual journal
in hand. "I want to show you something," he said. He
opened his journal to a particular entry with five specific goals that he had decided were necessary to cause him
to experience spiritual victory. The list included spending thirty minutes in prayer each day, reading five chapters of the Bible, leading a daily devotional time for his
family, giving materially to someone every week, and
witnessing each day. "I consider these things to be basic
to the Christian life," he explained, "but I can't even do
this consistently. What can I do to motivate myself to be
faithful in these areas?" Mark had his neat list of commandments that he believed he must obey to be victorious. Yet he viewed the commandments from a perspective of law, not grace.

Do you remember what law does to a person? It
arouses sinful passions; consequently, Mark couldn't
obey these basic commands. As a result, he was experiencing major anxiety. This is how it always is with a

legalist. He views the commands of the New Testament with a sense of guilt and self-condemnation. He can never do enough to please God. Even if Mark had been able to successfully obey the commands he thought most important, he still would have been frustrated. The one word that law will never say is "enough." That's why legalists can never be satisfied. They grasp for more and more rules, trying in vain to find fulfillment through behavior. No matter how much they do, it's never enough.

There is a better way to view the New Testament commands. As you move forward into the grace walk, a mental shift takes place which causes you to begin to see the commandments in a positive way. You begin to understand them from a basis of love. "For this is the love of God, that we keep His commandments. And His commandments are not burdensome" (1 John 5:3).

A grace perspective lets us see the commands not as obligations, but as opportunities for the life of Christ to be revealed through us. We *want* to respond in obedience to them because the commandments are a beautiful picture of the many ways that Christ's life can be seen through our lifestyle. Set free by grace, we don't face the commandments with self-condemnation, but with spiritual anticipation that Jesus Christ will reveal His life in us. Jesus didn't break the Law 2,000 years ago, but rather fulfilled it. As He lives His life through us today, *He* will fulfill the commands of the New Testament. The Christian *abides* in Christ, *chooses* to obey His commandments, and then *acts in faith*. Every commandment is another way that Christ can be seen in us!

Are you struggling for victory in your Christian life? Don't focus on the commandments as a doorway to victory. *Christ* is your victory! As you learn to abide in Him and He expresses His life through you, the commandments will become a blessing, not a burden. You will experience the joy of walking in grace, not guilt.

Jesus said, "If you love Me, you will keep My commandments" (John 14:15, NASB). When I was a legalist, I read this verse to say, "Keep My commandments to show that you love Me." That understanding left me trying to do what He said in order to demonstrate that I loved Him. However, that is not what the verse says. Jesus said that if we love Him, we *will* keep His commandments. Do you see the difference? One approach translates into a burden, while the other is a release from struggling. Failure to keep the commandments is a symptom of the problem, not the problem itself. The real issue in disobedience is a love problem. If we wrestle with being consistently obedient, the remedy for the problem is to love Him more! However, that answer raises another question. *How* do we grow in our love for our Heavenly Father?

To Know Him Is to Love Him

Imagine Jesus physically coming into the room where you are now. He walks over to where you sit and the two of you begin to talk. As He is turning to leave the room, you say, "Jesus, before You leave, please allow me to ask one question. I've spent a great deal of time and energy on different things in this world. Now I want the rest of my time on this earth to really count. What one commandment is more important to you than anything else?"

What do you suppose He would answer? It isn't necessary to guess the answer because someone did ask Him that question during His earthly ministry. A religious leader asked, "'Teacher, which is the great commandment in the law?' Jesus said to him, 'You shall love the LORD your God with all your heart, with all your soul, and with all your mind. This is the first and great commandment'" (Matthew 22:36-38).

When asked which is the greatest commandment God has given, Jesus said that it is to love Him. A person's love for God is directly proportionate to their knowledge of Him. This is why knowing Him intimately is of supreme importance. A main concern of Jesus immediately before He was arrested and separated from His disciples was that they should have a deep love for the Father. Consider the final words of His prayer in the Upper Room at the last supper.

> O righteous Father! The world has not known You, but I have known You; and these have known that You sent Me. And I have declared to them Your name, and will declare it, that the love with which You loved Me may be in them, and I in them (John 17:25-26).

Jesus said that He had declared the name of the Father to the disciples so that they might share in the love that exists between the Father and the Son. To declare the Father's name literally means to reveal His character. It was the goal of Jesus to reveal the Father so that the love of the Father and Son would be in the disciples too.

The ministry of the Holy Spirit today is to reveal God's nature, in order that we might enter into a Divine love relationship. If you feel weak in your love for your Heavenly Father, ask the Holy Spirit to more fully reveal Him to you each day through every circumstance that comes into your life. If you are hungry to know God, He will make Himself known to you! As you come to know Him more, you will love Him more. My concept of God has changed since I have come to better understand His grace. Whereas before, I saw Him as a God who demanded my love, now I see Him as Someone I can't help but love, as I come to know Him better. He really is lovable!

CHAPTER 10

FROM DUTY
TO DELIGHT

G race has changed the way I look at some aspects of a Christian lifestyle. Knowing that I am free from fulfilling certain "Christian duties" has actually released me to do those things. When I was a legalist I was never *free* because I felt *obligated* to do them. Self-imposed laws gave me no choice in the matter. A system of Christian rules which I read into the Bible dictated my responsibility.

Perhaps you too have been conditioned to view certain aspects of the Christian life as your spiritual duty. As you move into the grace walk, you will see how grace elevates these same responsibilities to the place of privilege and delight. Depending on our background, each of us have specific ideas about the obligations inherent to the Christian life. My own tradition dictated that I perform well in several areas which I considered to be an integral part of a successful Christian lifestyle.

Living by the Bible

When I was young, someone gave me a Bible with

these words written on the first page: "This Book will keep you from sin and sin will keep you from this Book." It made sense to me. However I began to find that it wasn't quite that simple. Sin would certainly keep me from the Book, but the Book wouldn't necessarily keep me from sin.

There are two things teenaged boys think about all the time. One of them is cars and the other is girls. Boys don't often get into trouble thinking about cars, but girls are a different matter. Raging hormones and an active imagination are the plight of the teen years. When I was in that pubescent stage, I read a book on how to handle the devil when he tempts you. The author suggested identifying your weaknesses and then recording on index cards verses from the Bible that address the particular area of vulnerability. Then when the devil tempts you, pull out your sword and chop his head off. So that's what I did. I set out with my pocket full of cards, each with verses relevant to the potential pitfalls of my youthfulness. One card eventually became worn and bent more than all the others. It contained a verse found in 1 Peter 2:11. "Dearly beloved, I beseech you as strangers and pilgrims, abstain from fleshly lusts which war against the soul" (KJV). For a boy at puberty, the whole world is a girl. When I found my thoughts racing down the tracks of the Eros Express, I would pull out my card and read it out loud, as if to ward off the evil spirits that were pulling me down the tracks. Yet it didn't stop the locomotive of lust. Later after the train had run its course and had pulled into the terminal, I was overwhelmed with a sense of condemnation. *I'm scum,* I would think to myself. *God will never be able to use me.* I often wondered why the Bible didn't seem to help me at those times.

As the years passed, the framework for temptation changed, but my approach to dealing with it would remain the same. I did throw away the index cards, but I still determined to live by the Bible. It was only after I began to understand grace that I realized that God never intended that we should live by the Bible. We are to live by His life. I wanted to build my lifestyle around the teachings of the Bible, which is nothing more than embracing a *biblical* value system. Do you remember what we discussed in chapter 8? God doesn't want us to live by a value system. The Bible *is* a weapon against the powers of darkness. However it isn't possible to recite verses to the devil and expect him to run in fear. Remember that Satan himself quoted the Bible, when he tempted Jesus in the wilderness. The Bible is a weapon against sin when it is internalized together with a sincere love for Christ. Memorizing Scripture loads the gun, but only love can pull the trigger. I realize now that as a youth I pointed the gun at the devil and shouted, "Bang! Bang!" It's no wonder he didn't drop. God still had to teach me some things about loving Him. As you abide in Christ moment by moment, your love for Him will enable you to resist temptation by the power of His life within you. Failure to rest in Him leaves you with nothing more than your own willpower to resist temptation. Self-sufficiency against temptation is a one-sided fight!

Learning the Bible

There is another misconception about the Bible that an understanding of grace corrects. We know that learning the contents of the Bible is important, but why? A performance-based Christian often studies the Bible to gain information. This approach to Bible study is generally unprofitable and can also be dangerous. Gaining knowledge just for the sake of knowing more of the Bible is actually harmful. Paul plainly said that "knowledge puffs up." The modern church is filled with Christians who race from one Bible conference to another to gain knowledge. Christian television and radio stations flourish. Study notes on the Bible abound. There is no lack of information about the Bible. Yet I wonder if there have ever been more worldly minded believers in the church.

A legalistic approach to the Bible carries one to its pages for *information;* grace brings the believer to the Bible seeking *revelation.* I once heard of a church that was against pastors having seminary training. The pastor prayed, "I want to thank You, Lord, for my ignorance." A member chimed in, "Bless him, Lord. He has a lot to be thankful for." I am certainly not suggesting that ignorance of the Scripture is a virtue. But biblical information without revelation is empty religion!

It's possible to excel in academic knowledge of the Bible and not experience the life of Christ. One might parse Greek verbs and miss the very presence of Jesus! I have often heard the Bible compared to a love letter. It's a good comparison. A grace-oriented method of Bible study creates a hunger to know Jesus and to hear His voice.

Not long ago I participated in a men's retreat that lasted several days. On the first night there, as I prepared to go to bed, I found a love note that Melanie had stuck in the case with my toothbrush and razor. I read the note and smiled. The next morning I found another note she had placed under my shirt. That evening, another note. Same thing the next day. With each passing day, the notes became more mushy. Finally, on the last day I found one she had hidden in my suit pocket. This one was the clincher—it had her perfume sprinkled on it. What effect do you think these notes had on me? What would you think if I told you that I pasted them all on a piece of posterboard? Then when I arrived at home, I ignored my wife and went to my room and hung the posterboard on the wall so I could read the notes every day. You would think I'd lost my mind, wouldn't you? The letters were great, but they only served to draw my emotion and devotion toward her.

That's what the Holy Spirit does when we approach the Bible with a grace perspective. He uses the inspired Word to reveal a loving God to us and to create within us a desire to know Him more intimately. Grace personalizes the Bible and causes it to become to us subjectively what it already is objectively—the inspired word of God to us as individuals. Legalists can talk all day about the Bible being the Word of God, but legalism deafens us to God's voice. Only grace can cause the deaf to hear God as He speaks through His Word. I have always believed that the Bible is inerrant, but now I know it is much more than that. It is alive with the very expression of Divine Life!

Have You Had Your Quiet Time Today?

Another area of my life that has dramatically changed since beginning the grace walk is my prayer life. One of the most difficult aspects of my Christian lifestyle before appropriating Christ as life was consistency in spending time "alone with God." I called it my quiet time and that is often what it was—quiet. In fact, a few times it became so quiet that I fell asleep! Legalism turns prayer into a boring monologue, while grace turns it into a delightful conversation. Is your prayer life characterized by routine and repetition? It startled me when those words described my prayer life and I came to realize that was the kind of prayer life the Pharisees had! I don't *say* prayers anymore. I just pray.

When our daughter Amy was a small child, we were putting her to bed one night and were ready to "say her prayers" with her. We knelt beside her bed and she prayed, "God is great, God is good, let us thank Him for our food." She paused, looked up at us and said, "I think I said the wrong prayer." Right. I've seen adults do it many times too. I've done it myself. The same phrases said in the same way at the same time in the same place. I remember as a kid hearing people always pray for "the boys in Vietnam." When the war finally ended and they came home, one guy kept right on praying for "the boys in Vietnam." Even then I wondered if anyone had told him that the war was over.

I know these are exaggerated examples, but the point is the ease with which we fall into a rut when our prayers stem from duty and not from an intimate relationship with Christ. Grace changes our concept of the nature of prayer. It stimulates a continuing prayer *relationship* as opposed to a daily prayer routine.

When Sarah comes home from work, she goes through the same routine. She greets her husband with a peck on his cheek. Then she affirms him in some way, often using the same words. Next she asks him to do any particular thing that she might want done that evening. Then she talks to him about the kids and their problems or needs. That discussion is always followed by a time when she asks his opinion on decisions that she might be facing. She pretty much has her mind made up already, but she wants his approval on her decision. Finally, she thanks him for everything he does for her and promises to do her best to be the right kind of wife. She follows this exact routine every day, even though her heart isn't in it most of the time. This habit takes about thirty minutes. After that she pretty much ignores her husband the rest of the evening.

What kind of relationship do you think Sarah has with her husband? I confess that Sarah is an imaginary character. If a wife did discipline herself to communicate with her husband in this way, she wouldn't find much intimacy in the relationship. Yet this scenario is an accurate picture of the prayer life of many Christians. They determine to pray at the same time in the same way every day. Their prayer life is built around a formula which includes four or five steps which they believe one must take in prayer. They discipline themselves to this routine, whether their heart is in it or not. I challenge you to seriously ask yourself, is this really the kind of communication God wants from His bride?

Before I understood grace, my prayer life could be characterized as something I *did*, an *action* that occurred when I spoke to God. Now prayer is different. It's still an action, but it is much more than that. It is an *attitude*. It is an open communion with the Father at every mo-ment I am abiding in Christ. This is the only thing that could be meant by the biblical injunction, "Pray with-out ceasing." Are we to walk around communicating with God using words at every second of the day? To pray without ceasing is to communicate with God at every moment. Sometimes words are necessary; at other times they aren't.

Our kids say that Melanie and I sometimes talk without speaking. They're right. They have suggested that we often read each other's mind. That's not altogether wrong either. We have been married twenty-two years, and we *do* know each other's mind fairly well. Sometimes speaking isn't necessary—a glance may be sufficient. Volumes can be communicated by silence. I'm not uncomfortable when Melanie isn't talking to me, unless I sense that there is a *reason* she isn't speaking. If that's the case, I want to find out why and resolve the matter. Otherwise, silence is comfortable.

When we first began to date as teens, I felt a need to talk all the time; but as we have grown in intimacy, that isn't necessary. Do we talk? Yes, often and intimately. Do we set aside thirty minutes a day for our "quiet time" together so that we can talk to each other? I can't imagine us sitting down during a thirty-minute period that we've blocked out for that purpose and saying, "Okay, let's talk. I'll go first." That would be awkward and forced. It wouldn't feel natural. I'd rather just yell, "Hey, listen to this," to the kitchen when I want to read "Dear Abby" to her or tell her about something on the news right then. I'd rather have her just tell me what she's thinking with spontaneity, not with some agenda for conversation that she has planned.

I'm not suggesting that it's improper to have a designated time to pray, if that's what you *want* to do. I am saying that a disciplined quiet time with no real life in it is pointless. As you move forward in the grace walk, you'll begin to see prayer more as a lifestyle than a spiritual discipline. You will find yourself talking to your Father dozens of times a day, not just during a designated prayer time. You'll talk to Him about important things and incidental things. Someone said that they don't bother talking to God about the small things because He's so busy. Remember this—*it's all small to God!* He doesn't need to conserve His energy for the big stuff. He is omnipotent! You won't drain Him of His power. If He knows how many hairs are on your head,

He must care about every single detail of your life, regardless of how small it may seem to you.

Hearing the Voice of God

Another aspect of prayer in a grace-oriented lifestyle is that God talks back. God spoke to people in the Bible in many ways. There's no way to say how He may speak to you, but He *will* speak as you learn to relate to Him through grace, instead of trying to relate through your Christian performance. God has never spoken to me audibly, but at times He has spoken louder than that. Do you expect God to speak to you as you pray and read His Word? Many modern Christians never expect to actually hear God's voice personally. Jack Taylor writes about their expectation of silence:

> The hovering heresy is the notion that God used to be *articulate* and *active* and is now *mute* and *motionless.* It is the idea that since God gave us a Book, He does not need to communicate with His world anymore.
>
> Does that sound farfetched to you? Are you aware that much of the church today possesses a spiritual worldview in line with this mentality?
>
> You say, "I don't know anyone who would make such a claim." While that may be true, there are many believers today who live close to the edge of that heresy.
>
> It seems to have emerged soon after the canon of Scripture was finished. "Since the Bible is the Word of God," some reasoned, "God has had His say and that is that. What He has spoken is both perfect and complete.

> We have all the revelation we will ever need."
> And this silent supposition (that God has fin-
> ished with speaking) floats around the church
> today largely unchallenged.[1]

The Bible concordance on my computer indicates that the phrase "saith the LORD" is found in the Bible 577 times, and "the LORD spake" 143 times. That's a total of 720 times that the Bible says God directly spoke. Do you hear His voice? Jesus said that His sheep would know His voice, but some Christians never expect to hear it again after they are saved. God's desire is to fellowship with His children in an ongoing dialogue. Grace opens a person's ears to hear God in a way that legalism will never allow. As a legalist, I focused on knowing what God wanted me to do. In the grace walk, I have experienced a growing desire to know God—period. As I have come to know Him more intimately, I have discovered what He wants me to do without the struggles that once characterized my performance-based lifestyle. God's will is not primarily a *path*, but a *Person* named Jesus Christ. As we abide in Him, it is *impossible* to miss the will of God, because His very life is being expressed through us at every moment.

When a Christian abides in Christ, he can assume that his thoughts and decisions are being directed by the Holy Spirit within him. Perhaps no man has been more mightily used by God than the apostle Paul. Yet there is no evidence that he spent time agonizing over where he should go and what he should do. He didn't struggle to know the will of God, but just *did* the will of God each day. His attitude is seen in 1 Corinthians 2:16 where he asserts, "But we have the mind of Christ." Paul's actions revolved around doing what came naturally.

It should be clear by now that the natural thing for saints is to glorify God through our lifestyle. If we are abiding in Christ, then He is expressing His life through us each moment. Satan wants us to believe that it is easy to get out of the will of God. Yet if we are abiding in Christ, it is impossible to get out of His will. How can we get out of the will of God if Christ is expressing His life through us moment by moment? On the other hand, if we are not abiding in Christ, our actions can't possibly have any godly value, because we are acting out of the flesh instead of faith.

I explained this truth to Jim one day when he was agonizing over the decision of whether he should accept a job offer. "I don't want to do the wrong thing," he said. I explained to him from the Scriptures that he had the mind of Christ; if he was resting in Christ, he could trust his thoughts as being from Him. "If that's true, it sure would take a load off my mind," Jim responded. It was exciting to see Jim come to realize that it *is* true! As believers abide in Christ, they can act in confidence that the Holy Spirit will guide every thought and deed. Christians need to give as much credit to God's ability to lead as they give to the ability of Satan to mislead!

Grace takes the responsibility of knowing the will of God off of us and places it on Him. This is liberating. Under law, one must *find* the will of God. In the grace walk, the will of God is *revealed* by the Holy Spirit to the believer, whose only responsibility is to rest in Him. God does speak to us today to make His will known. Occasionally He speaks in ways that seem almost sensational, but don't discount the many times that God may speak through our thought process. When our focus in prayer is only to gain information from God so that we can make a right decision, our prayer life will be frustrating. But when our focus in prayer is to experience the reality of fellowship with God, the specific decisions we must make will become apparent. Grace allows abiding believers to act in confidence that a sovereign God above is directing our circumstances, that a supernatural Spirit within is directing our thoughts, and that an omniscient Christ is expressing His life through us. It is foolish to worry about making the wrong choice when we have that kind of support working on our behalf!

Bible study and prayer were a *discipline* to me as a legalist. My thesaurus suggests these synonyms for discipline: "chastisement, control, order, or restraint." It's no wonder I found it hard to be consistent in these areas! But grace has turned it into a *delight*. The same thesaurus suggests synonyms for delight: "enjoyment, pleasure, happiness, and joy." Which approach do you prefer, a legalist or grace approach?

Time spent in the Bible and prayer have to do with the way I relate to God. Grace has dramatically affected that vertical relationship, but that's not all it has done. Learning to walk in grace is affecting the way I relate to those around me too. Learning to relate to God through grace will cause a Christian to begin to relate to others on the basis of grace, opening the way to give and receive love in a way that is nothing less than supernatural.

CHAPTER 11

PEOPLE WHO NEED PEOPLE

U nderstanding Christ as life has been the most thrilling spiritual truth that I have ever realized. Yet God's purpose in revealing this exchanged life to His children is not simply so that we will enjoy the grace walk. His ultimate purpose is that He might reveal Himself in this world through those who abide in Him. To express His life through believers is the ultimate intention of the Father. It is as we fulfill His divine purpose that we find our greatest contentment.

If you had one son in whom you found unspeakable delight, would it not be normal as a father to want many more? It is exactly so with the eternal Father, who by nature and choice, has desired and purposed to have a vast family of human-divine sons who are just like His only begotten Son.

Further, as we view from His heart, it seems evident that the Father makes all His

plans with His eternal Son in view; that in the
unfolding ages ahead, Jesus Christ might have
a glorious Body in which to express His very
life, and a family of brothers with whom He
might enjoy fellowship.

Then as we understand the innermost purpose of the Son, we see how in turn He dedicates Himself to helping the Father realize His
intention for Himself; that He (the Father)
might have a family of sons in whom He can
have paternal honor, glory, pleasure and
delight. The Father plans for His Son, whereas the Son lives unto the Father.

So it is in the Godhead. In a sense no member lives *for* or *unto Himself*, but each for the
Other. The Father intends that in all things
the Son might have preeminence. The Son
lives to reveal the Father and thus brings glory
and pleasure to Him. Likewise the Spirit
speaks not of Himself (nor for Himself) but
dedicates His activity to the revealing of the
Son and to realizing for both the Father and
the Son.[1]

The life pattern of believers is shown in the way that
the Father, Son, and Holy Spirit relate to each other.
Each seeks to minister to the other. So it is to be with
the church of Jesus Christ in this world. There is no
such thing as Christianity turned inward. Empty religion seeks to preserve itself and focuses on *gathering*.
New Testament Christianity purposes to *pour itself out*
in ministry to others. The ultimate benefit in allowing
Christ to express His life through us is not what happens
in us personally. Personal fulfillment is a wonderful by-

product of His life within, but His greater goal is to express His life to a needy world through loving ministry.

Legalistic religion promises freedom, but actually causes those who are drawn into its snare to become prisoners of rules. Grace causes the Christian to simply rest in Christ, allowing Him to reveal Himself to others in the course of living each day naturally. Religion makes performance its priority. Grace chooses people as its priority. It frees us to take our eyes off ourselves and allows us to invest ourselves in others. It is a freedom which activates ministry motivated by life, not laws. Law *insists* on ministry. Grace *inspires* it.

Since coming to understand Christ as Life, I have related to people in a different way. As you proceed in the grace walk, you may also discover this change. Jesus loved people during his earthly ministry 2,000 years ago. He still loves them and will express that love through you as you rest in Him.

Evangelism in Grace

It has been absolutely liberating to understand evangelism from a grace perspective. There have been several notable differences in my approach to evangelism since coming to understand the wonder of resting in Him.

• *Grace causes one to see people instead of prospects.* Words have different connotations to each person who hears them. The word "prospect" has pretty much dropped out of my vocabulary in reference to evangelism. As a legalist, I classified people as "prospects for salvation" or "prospects for church membership." I know it's just a word, but to me it depersonalizes people. I'm not trying to convince you to drop the word, but to see the distinction between two ways we may view unsaved people. When unbelievers are just prospects, evangelism becomes utilitarian, as people are seen as resources for building the church. A grace-oriented outlook sees unbelievers as people who are hungry to experience Christ's love.

Carried to its extreme, a legalistic approach to evangelism can become worldly. When I was in my mid-twenties, I emphasized professions of faith and baptisms above everything else. We talked about reaching people; but in retrospect I wonder how many people a church reaches when they come in the front door, pass through the baptistry, and then exit out the back door within a matter of months. Another young pastor and I agreed that our churches would compete in the number of baptisms we could have in a twelve-week period. We were sincere. I suppose I'm not the first person to do something sincerely foolish. For twelve weeks I pushed for baptisms like the end of the world was coming. I would baptize anybody who would repeat "the sinner's prayer" with me. We baptized bus kids as if they were on a sanctified conveyor belt. We baptized some adults. I thought of counting the fat ones as two baptisms or maybe double-dipping some of them. I'm kidding, of course, but it's embarrassing to reflect on those days. While my experience may not be the norm, the attitude that demands we reach numbers of people at all costs is not uncommon.

I have become convinced that people enter and exit our modern churches because *we fail to connect with them as people.* They just move up on our prospect list. Once they are no longer prospects for salvation or church membership, they become prospects for being teacher, choir member, deacon, or elder. Grace changes that. In the grace walk, we see people in the light of relationship instead of resources.

• *Grace makes evangelism a real joy instead of a religious job.* Sheree and I were talking about evangelism when she remarked, "For the first time in my Christian life, I *want* to tell people about the Lord. Before I understood grace, I didn't have any motivation to witness. I felt guilty because I knew that I should, but I didn't want to witness." There are two reasons why Sheree's opinion on witnessing changed.

The first reason she found it hard to witness is one that all evangelicals have faced. A law among evangelicals and fundamentalists insists that we must evangelize. This brings us back to what has already been discussed, namely that law motivates a person to do exactly opposite from what it demands. Understanding that she isn't duty-bound to witness has given Sheree the freedom to do it because she wants to.

The second reason Sheree found it hard to witness is that she couldn't get excited about enlisting people to join the kind of performance-based Christian lifestyle that drains so much out of a person. However, when she discovered grace for the Christian, she knew that kind of life is worth offering to others because it is invigorating and exciting. Her motivation now is to allow Christ to express His life through her as she goes about her normal activities. Sharing Christ has become natural instead of forced.

The evangelism of the early church was a continuous and spontaneous expression of Christ's life within them. The church of the twentieth century may stress the need for an effective evangelism program, but the church of the New Testament had no such concept. Evangelism wasn't a program to those Christians—it was a way of life. A Christian who didn't evangelize would have been like a farmer who didn't plant, or a soldier who didn't fight. The church at Jerusalem didn't need to be motivated to witness. On the contrary, it couldn't be stopped.

When Peter and John were arrested for preaching and teaching, they were carried before the Sanhedrin where they were severely threatened and warned not to speak at all in the name of Jesus. "But Peter and John answered and said to them, 'Whether it is right in the sight of God to listen to you more than to God, you judge. For we cannot but speak the things which we have seen and heard' " (Acts 4:19-20).

When people are consumed with desire, they can't be stopped! Grace inflames the desire to witness. It ignites compassion toward the lost and motivates Christians to naturally witness with supernatural power. Grace-based evangelism is nothing less than an excitement about Jesus that is contagious to others.

• *Grace motivates one to share a Person, not a plan.* When I was a legalist, my focus toward the lost was on sharing "the plan of salvation." I began by asking the question, "If you were to die today, do you know where you would spend eternity?" If they didn't give the right answer with confidence, I would proceed to share a four-point plan from the Bible. At the end of the presentation, the person would be asked to make a decision for Christ.

I don't want to be misunderstood at this point. It *is* important to share the Word with unbelievers as we witness to them about Christ. I know that faith comes by hearing the Word of God. In no way do I intend to minimize the role of Scripture in evangelism. Yet it is possible to share a "plan" of salvation without making it clear that we are seeking to introduce the lost person to Christ. The goal of evangelism is not to obtain decisions *for* Christ, but to introduce people *to* Christ.

Effective evangelism doesn't simply leave a person with the *knowledge* that he is a Christian. Thorough evangelism leaves him *in love* with a Person named Jesus. It offers the new Christian an understanding that his identity has changed through his relationship to Christ. What assurance does the new believer have that he has really been saved? If he was evangelized through a plan of salvation which *ended* with an opportunity for a decision, his only basis for assurance is by looking back to the moment when he made his decision for Christ. If he was made aware that he was entering into an eternal relationship with the living Christ, his assurance of salvation is that he *knows* Christ *right now*.

If I were to awaken tomorrow morning with amnesia, I am convinced that I would know I am a Christian because of the conscious presence of Christ within me. I'm glad I remember trusting Christ when I was eight years old, but the greatest joy of my Christian life is not found in pointing back to what happened when I was eight. The greatest joy is to experience the presence of God through Christ right now! It's no wonder that some Christians aren't very excited about their faith. It's tough to stay enthused about something that happened years ago. However, it isn't hard to stay delighted with an intimate daily love relationship with the God of this universe! Grace stresses our relationship to a Person, not our response to a plan.

• *Grace-oriented evangelism offers life, not just forgiveness.* Most of the contemporary approaches to evangelism stress the importance of receiving forgiveness of sin so that a person might go to heaven when he dies. Yet this is not God's primary goal in offering salvation. His main objective in reaching out to us is to share His Life with us. Forgiveness clears the way for us to enter heaven, but forgiveness alone can do nothing to make new people out of us today. In His mercy, God extends forgiveness, but grace does much more than provide forgiveness.

Some years ago I read Elizabeth Elliot's account of the brutal slaying of her missionary husband, Jim Elliot, by a tribe of Auca Indians. He and four other young missionaries had gone to great lengths to win the confidence of those barbaric people in hopes of sharing the gospel with them, but they were murdered in cold blood as they reached out in love to this tribe. Elizabeth Elliot's forgiveness toward the men who participated in the death of her husband is nothing less than a divine response to inhumanity. To forgive them is to extend mercy. Yet she went beyond mercy in her response to this horror. She moved into the Indian village where those who took her husband from her lived and reached out to the people in forgiveness. Not only did she express her forgiveness to them, but she found the very man who had taken her husband's life and expressed *love* to him. I saw a picture of her giving a haircut to the man who murdered Jim Elliot. Now *that* is grace! Mercy doesn't give us what we *do* deserve—justice. Grace goes far beyond mercy. Grace offers us what we *don't* deserve—lavishing lovingkindness.

It was because of our sin that Christ died; yet, God offers forgiveness to those who will receive it. That's wonderful. We will never be accountable for our sin because Christ took upon Himself God's wrath against sin. *That is mercy.* Through Christ we are offered life—joyful, abundant, exhilarating, divine, eternal life! *That is grace!*

Evangelism that presents only the opportunity for forgiveness falls short of all that God offers. Forgiveness is a necessary but secondary step toward the main goal, which is to receive and experience Divine Life! A grace-based evangelism won't stop at an explanation of redemption for the purpose of forgiveness alone.

> Redemption is big enough, wonderful enough, to occupy a very large place in our vision; but God is saying that we should not make redemption to be everything, as though man were created to be redeemed. The Fall is indeed a tragic dip downwards in that line of purpose, and the atonement a blessed recovery whereby our sins are blotted out and we are restored; but when it is accomplished there yet remains a work to be done to bring us into possession of that which Adam never possessed, and to give God that which His heart desires. For God has never forsaken the purpose which is represented by that straight line.
>
> Believers are prone to allow God's *recovery work* to overshadow His *realizing work.* We absolutely must see both in their proper place. Because of man's perverted tendencies toward self-relating, he has been more alive to *what God does for him,* than to *what he is destined to be unto God.* Our present lesson brings both aspects of God's work into view: (1) Through

the cross the work of the devil was destroyed; redemption and release from the bondage of sin and the effect of the Fall were provided, and: (2) Through the cross provision was made whereby man can once again live to realize the Father's ultimate intention.[2]

God's ultimate intention is to express His life through us. As I have grown in my understanding of grace, I have experienced an increasing desire to share His life with those who aren't saved. I explain to them that through Christ, *God will forgive their sins so that He might give them His life.* Too many nominal Christians endure mundane lives, because their understanding of the Christian life revolves around being forgiven and going to heaven. What would happen if the modern church became fully aware of the truth that Christ lives in them and wants to express His life through them? The church described in the Book of Acts stressed this truth in evangelism, and in a short time the whole known world had heard about Jesus of Nazareth. Modern evangelism has continued to present forgiveness, but generally ignores the aspect of receiving divine life at salvation. The results of this omission can be measured by noting the difference between the evangelistic fervor of the ancient and modern church.

Grace and the Church

There is a picture on my office wall that I find fascinating. It is a computer-generated picture of various shades of color blended into dark lines. It resembles what a canvas might look like if a very large tire was dipped into many colors of paint and then rolled over it. The color and design have an aesthetic beauty even though there is no discernable design to the casual observer. At the bottom of the print is the title, "Nature's Majesty." The fascinating aspect of this print is the three-dimensional picture within the colors and lines. When I first saw this print in the store, I saw nothing intelligible about it. The clerk suggested that I could see the hidden picture if I looked at my own reflection in the glass that covered the print. By staring at my own reflection, she said that I would double the distance of my focus and the three-dimensional image would emerge. I stood there for a while, wondering if someone was making a fool out of me, when suddenly the picture began to appear just as she said it would. In the center of the print is a large eagle with its wings outstretched. It holds a fish in its claw and is descending upon a nest where two baby birds eagerly stretch their heads upward to receive food. Once you see it it's perfectly clear. I've shown it to a few friends who have stared at it for a long time and just can't see it. Others look in puzzlement for a while, then begin to smile in amazement as the eagle appears in focus.

This picture illustrates what grace has done to my perception of the church. I have been within the walls where the church meets since I was a young child. I have long recognized its distinct colors and lines. Yet grace has changed the church from a two-dimensional print into a three-dimensional work of art. The beauty of the church has appeared as I have continued to look at the reflection of Christ in His church. While I saw some aesthetic beauty in the church before I began experiencing the grace walk, its beauty was flat compared to the three-dimensional work of divine art that has materialized before my eyes since coming to understand Christ as life.

God's Church Is a Showcase of Grace

The church is more than a group of people who have all been born again. The church consists of God's trophies of grace. In this world and throughout the ages, every Christian is a testimony to the loving grace of the Father. The apostle Paul said:

> But God, who is rich in mercy, because of His great love with which He loved us, even when we were dead in trespasses, made us alive together with Christ (by grace you have been saved), and raised us up together, and made us sit together in the heavenly places in Christ Jesus, that in the ages to come He might show the exceeding riches of His grace in His kindness toward us in Christ Jesus (Ephesians 2:4-7).

Throughout eternity, God will be glorified because He has extended His kindness toward us through Christ Jesus. We certainly didn't deserve His grace, yet He *chose* to extend loving grace toward us on the basis of His own loving nature.

Unlike their Father, performance-based Christians accept other people according to their conduct. One walking in grace accepts people on the basis of unconditional love. This doesn't suggest a blanket approval of all behavior, but grace allows one to accept and love others regardless of their actions. Legalists set out to change what people *do*. Grace looks beyond what others do and affirms them for who they *are*, encouraging them to live up to their identity. Legalists heap guilt and shame on those who fail to measure up. A gracious Christian loves unconditionally.

As you extend grace to Christians who stumble and fail, you will be amazed at the impact it has on their life. A Christian who has fallen doesn't need condemnation. He probably already has enough self-condemnation to cause him to feel crushed under its weight. Condemnation of a believer *never* comes from God. The Bible clearly teaches that there is no condemnation to those who are in Christ (Romans 8:1). If God doesn't condemn His children, who are we to condemn each other?

Rick told me that he felt like God had abandoned him lately. His demeanor was stoic, bordering on anger.

"What's going on inside you right now?" I asked.

"It seems like God has forgotten me. I feel empty and cold."

As I listened to Rick express his pain and acknowledged the validity of his feelings, I could see him begin to mellow a little. Finally, I began to share the truth.

"Rick, God hasn't forgotten you. I can assure you of that. In fact, you are on His mind all the time. He *delights* in you."

He broke eye contact with me and looked down at the floor. In the minutes that followed, I assured him of how much he is loved and accepted by his Heavenly Father.

"You say that God accepts me, but you don't know all the details," Rick responded. Then the heart of the matter came out. Rick confessed that he had been enslaved to pornographic movies in hotel rooms where he stayed when out of town on business. His voice trembled as he described his struggle to resist this temptation when he was alone.

"Rick, God doesn't accept you because you do the right things and He doesn't stop accepting you when you do the wrong things." I explained that God's love and acceptance of him was because of who he is *in Christ*. We talked about the matter of identity.

"The reason you feel such anxiety right now is because you are acting in a way that is inconsistent with who you are," I explained.

I met with Rick for several weeks, sharing with him the truth of his identity in Christ. Once he discovered his true identity, he began to find freedom over his habitual temptation. One day he acknowledged, "Steve, last week when I was out of town, I dealt with some stressful situations at work. That night at the hotel, the urge to turn on the porn was strong. I gave in and turned it on—for a little while. Then I realized that this wasn't what I wanted, so I turned it off. I really believe I'm free from it."

Rick's freedom didn't come through condemnation. His confession of sin was motivated by the affirmation of God's love and acceptance for him. Condemnation pushes us downward, telling us that we're no good. Conviction of sin is God's love in action toward His erring children, drawing our affection and devotion back toward the Father. In the process, we abandon the sins that plagued us.

The church isn't a company of sinlessly perfect people. Rather, it's a family of people whose lives demonstrate the transforming power of God's grace. One reason we need each other in the church family is to demonstrate our Father's unconditional love and acceptance. As we walk in grace, we will give others the same love and acceptance that we have received from God.

God's Church Is a Diverse Family

The three-dimensional picture in my office became

clear when I doubled the distance of my focus. The same principle applies to gaining a new perspective on the church. For many years, I viewed the church from a short distance. I am thankful for my own church heritage; my life has been immeasurably enriched through the fellowship of friends in the Christian tradition of which I have been a part. Yet a proper understanding of God's church requires that we step back from our own tree of traditions in order to see the whole forest.

Legalism is characterized by an attitude of exclusivity. It suggests that we are right in our position and others are wrong. Walking in grace has expanded my perception of the church. No group of Christians has a clear focus on all the truth. One group may have a better understanding of one part of the truth, while another group has a clearer understanding of another aspect of spiritual truth. That's why we need each other. Some have argued that all churches are right. If one insists on evaluating modern church life on the basis of right and wrong, then all Christian churches are right and all of them are wrong. In other words, no church or denomination is totally right or totally wrong. Embodied within the many denominations of the Christian community is the truth, but there is a great deal of superfluous dogma that conceals that truth from clear view.

I am not suggesting that doctrine is unimportant. The faithful church holds to indispensable tenets of belief. However, a grace perspective on the church doesn't demand that we all agree on every detail of faith and practice. I have never been a proponent of ecumenicism that throws doctrine out the church window; yet, there must be room somewhere within the structure of God's church for unity among the various members of the ecclesiastical family. Just because another brother may be different doesn't automatically make him wrong. A grace perspective allows diversity among the family of God.

In his first letter to the Corinthians, Paul uses the metaphor of the human body to illustrate the interdependence of the members of the body of Christ.

> For as the body is one and has many members, but all the members of that one body, being many, are one body, so also is Christ. For by one Spirit we were all baptized into one body—whether Jews or Greeks, whether slaves or free—and have all been made to drink into one Spirit (1 Corinthians 12:12-13).

We need each other! From God's perspective, His church is one body. Isn't that what Paul is saying? We have been joined together in union with Christ and with each other. We must recognize the distinctions within the members of the body and allow the Head to give direction to the various parts. Legalism wants to make every part of the body be a mouth or a foot or a hand, but the Word of God clearly teaches that each member of the body is responsible to follow the direction of the Head. Paul goes on to say, "But now God has set the members, each one of them, in the body just as He pleased. And if they were all one member, where would the body be? But now indeed there are many members, yet one body" (verses 18-20).

Watchman Nee writes about the orderly variety God intends in the church:

> Putting it bluntly, do not try to do everything and be everything yourself! No one in

his senses would desire to see the whole Body function merely in a single way. It is not reasonable for the whole to be an eye, nor for the eye to attempt the work of the whole. The Lord has ordered variety in the Body, an ear and a nose as well as an eye and a hand; not conformity, and certainly not single-organ monopoly.[3]

A grace-oriented understanding of the church will lead one to conclude that in reality there is only one church. The church is His body, under the direction of the Head. Every part of the body is dependent on the rest of the body to cooperate together to efficiently carry out the instructions from the Head. In His church, we *need* each other. Legalism separates Christians, but grace draws us together in a love relationship. We are one in union with Christ. Outward appearances may distinguish us from one another, but in essence we are the same because our very life is Christ.

CHAPTER 12

LIVING IN GRACE

ow can words even begin to adequately explain the wonders of a grace-filled life? I have written these chapters from my heart, including personal illustrations because I cannot separate the truths from their impact on my own life. I have understood the relationship between God's grace and unbelievers since I was a child. However, it has only been within the past few years that I have truly understood the grace of God in the life of believers. I don't just see things differently than I did before. I see things *new*. Understanding the truth that *Christ is my life* hasn't just changed my mind; it has transformed my life. The truths I have discussed in these pages don't outline what I believe; they embody who I am!

Occasionally I meet someone who talks about the exchanged life with an "us-them" mentality. Yet the very nature of grace makes it impossible for one who lives in grace to divide people into categories of "haves" and "have-nots." The revelation of Christ as one's life is *not* some second work of grace. It is simply a new awareness and appreciation for the life of Christ *which resides in every Christian.* There are no second-class Christians in God's family. We all have Christ within us, and when we possess His life, there is nothing more to be gained or desired!

In Plato's *The Republic* is "The Allegory of the Cave," a story told by Plato's teacher, Socrates. He used the story to illustrate the meaning of various degrees of knowledge and belief; the analogy also beautifully illustrates how God has worked with me to reveal Christ as my life. As you read this story, see if it applies to your life.

Imagine a cave, says Socrates, very far underground and with a long passage leading out into the daylight. In this cave there are men who have been prisoners there since they were children. They are chained to the ground, and even their heads are fastened in such a way that they can look only in front of them, at the wall of the cave. Behind the line of prisoners a fire is burning, and between the fire and the prisoners there is a roadway. People walk along this road and talk to one another and carry things with them. The prisoners would see the shadows of those people, shadows thrown by the light of the fire on the cave wall in front of them. And, supposing the cave wall reflected sound, the prisoners would hear sounds coming from the shadows. Since the prisoners cannot turn their heads, the only things they will see and know are shadows; and so they will assume that the shadows are *real things,* for they cannot know anything about the fire and the roadway and the people behind them.

Now, suppose we unchain one of the prisoners, and make him turn around. This will be very frightening and painful for him; the movements of his body will hurt him, and his eyes will be dazzled by the fire. And if we tell him that the things he now sees are more real than the shadows, he will not believe us, and he will want to sit down again and face the wall of the shadows which he understands. Now, suppose we go even further than this, and forcibly drag him out through the long tunnel into the sunlight. This will be even more painful and frightening for him; and when he arrives above the ground he will be blinded by the sun. But slowly, let us imagine, he will get used to it. At first, he will be able to look at the stars and the moon at night. Later he will look at shadows thrown by the sun and at reflections in pools of water. Finally, he will be able to see the trees and mountains in full daylight, and he will recognize that these, not the shadows in the cave, are the *real* things. And when he has become accustomed to looking around him, he will at last realize that the light which makes all this possible comes from the sun.[1]

The cave in this allegory represents one's frame of reference. I spent twenty-nine years of my Christian life living in the cave of legalism. Then the Holy Spirit lovingly began to take away those things that provided a sense of security for me—visible results in ministry and a sense of satisfaction in my Christian life. I now realize that those things which I so desperately clung to at the time were in reality nothing but chains which kept me from the light. In spite of my pain and fear, God pulled me away from what was familiar, and into the light of His grace. After several years, my eyes are still adjusting to the resplendent glory of grace. I am seeing more and more that routine religious performance is just a shadow. The substance of life is not in the shadows, but in the Son!

Once one has been freed from the cave, he can never interpret the shadows in the same way again. There is a whole world of grace to explore. Every day is an exciting adventure. Socrates contends that if the former prisoner were to be suddenly brought back into the cave, his eyes would be unaccustomed to the darkness, and he would no longer be able to recognize the shadows. His fellow prisoners would say that his experiences had ruined him, and they would consider him a fool for going out into the light.[2] Be prepared for the fact that as you leave the cave of legalism, not everybody will rejoice with you in your newfound freedom. Legalism has never walked peaceably with grace. Those who find their identity in religious performance bristle up at the suggestion that performance is only a shadow and not substance. The very suggestion of such a thing is perceived as an attack on their identity. Just remember, you are free! Walk in the light and enjoy your faith! While some will resent your freedom, others will be drawn up out of the cave into the light, as they see the joy you experience there.

Christ is *your* life. Grace and truth come through Him! (John 1:17). Yours is a life of grace. How can a life of grace be summarized? To even try to reduce the life of Christ to a few pages is impossible! But there are three characteristics of the grace-filled life that each of us should desire above all else.

Knowing Him

One of the most precious verses in my life will always be the one God spoke to me from Philippians 3:10 as I lay on the floor behind my desk, on that night I absolutely surrendered myself to Him to do *anything* He desired. From that night until this very moment, I have been consumed with the desire to know Him more intimately. It hasn't been an emotional desire at every moment, but a cognitive awareness that I want to *know* Him. I haven't lived every minute on the mountaintop where I started out, when I discovered that Christ is my life. I have walked through some valleys of frustration, disappointment, confusion, sins, and questions. I have experienced some highs and lows, and I have seen both my faith and my flesh at their strongest. Yet at each step there has been a foundational desire to know Him in increasing intimacy.

We will spend eternity getting to know our Heavenly Father. Can we be satisfied with the level of intimacy we have with Him today? Our present knowledge of Him is as one drop in an infinite ocean of knowledge. A deep knowledge of God won't come by biblical *education* alone, but through divine *revelation* as He chooses to open our eyes to understand Him more. God seldom reveals Himself to the casual and superficial Christian, but He is more than willing to make Himself known to those who have a genuine hunger for Him. We need to pray that God will do whatever is necessary to develop a hunger within us to *"know Him and the power of His resurrection, and the fellowship of His sufferings, being conformed to His death"* (Philippians 3:10).

Abiding in Him

One of the most liberating benefits in understanding grace is a freedom from the self-imposed mandate to be productive in measurable ways. There is absolutely nothing wrong with productivity being measurable. However striving to produce in order to be "successful" is wrong. Jesus said that we are simply branches who are to abide in the vine.

Fruit on the vine can do nothing to make itself grow. Apart from the vine, the branch has no life. The life of the vine *is* the life of the branch. Any fruit produced on the branch is the result of the life of the vine flowing through it. There is no jealousy between seedless and seeded grapes. No grape glories in its color, proud that it will produce wine with a better bouquet than others. None of the clusters compare themselves with other clusters to see how many grapes are in each group. No cluster argues that its group is closer to the vine than the others. This is beginning to sound ridiculous, but you get the point. Much of modern Christendom is obsessed with production at any cost. Some churches have given up on ever seeing a mighty rushing wind and have decided to settle for a whirlwind.

If you determine to simply abide in Christ, you will need to make a conscious decision to stand against the tide of modern opinion in the American religious world. Contemporary thought says, "Do something, even if it is wrong!" It is easy to mistake commotion for motion. However, the call of Christ to those who are His has not changed, *"Abide in Me."* Any person with a genuine desire to experience the Christ-life to the fullest cannot substitute *anything* for the quiet rest of abiding in Him daily. God will accomplish His purposes in our life according to His divine schedule. Grapes can't grow faster by grunting and groaning to produce growth. Andrew Murray rightly said:

> All the exercises of the spiritual life—our reading and praying, our willing and doing—have their very great value. But they can go no further than this, that they point the way and prepare us in humility to look to and depend upon God Himself, and in patience to wait for His good time and mercy.[3]

For the anxious Christian it is often easier to *do* something *for* God than to wait for God to do something *through* us. A life of grace is characterized by a calm confidence in a sovereign God whose love and wisdom always causes Him to do *what* He wants *when* He wants to do it. Inestimable damage may be done when we consciously or unconsciously try to move things forward, because God isn't moving fast enough for us.

Expressing Him

Abiding in Christ cannot be separated from expressing the life of Christ. Any grape which abides in the vine is both experiencing and expressing the life of the vine. Many want to produce an expression of Christian ministry without abiding in Him. The result is empty religious ritual which produces a ministry of death. When the "Christian religion" is *lacking the life of Christ*, it has no more power or status than any other religion. Don't miss the point. When the "Christian religion" is *lacking the life of Christ*, it ceases to be Christianity and becomes nothing more than a moral religion which teaches people how they should behave. Biblical Christianity *is* an expression of the life of Christ through His church in this world.

Can a person "practice Christianity" without being saved? No. They can *imitate* Christ's life to the best of their ability—a feeble attempt at best. Real Christianity is not an imitation, but an *expression* of Christ within us. Can a person who is saved imitate Christianity without expressing the life of Christ? Yes. Any effort to do something for God which comes from our own resources, ability, knowledge, etc. is flesh. Flesh can only counterfeit the real thing. The way to enjoy and express Christ is to allow Him to live His life through us. As we rest in Him, He will express His character and His ministry through us. When we struggle to live the Christian life, we stop the flow of Christ's life and begin to live after the resources of our own flesh. As we abide in Him, we rest and work at the same time! We rest inwardly while He works outwardly through us. This is God's designed method of Christian service. Anything else is empty religious ritual, regardless of how successful or spiritual it may appear.

Living in grace means that we express His life as a natural and normal part of our daily experience. We live trusting Him to express Himself through us every day. We don't have to overanalyze our actions and attitudes. Life isn't a test, it's a rest. The test has already been given and we received a perfect score because Jesus took the test for us. It's time now to celebrate! We don't need to live under a list of things we believe we ought to do. *When we are living each day abiding in Christ, we can do whatever we want to.* As we abide in Him, His desire will be our desire.

Some Christians have worry lines on their faces as deep as the bottomless pit. Lighten up! The Christ-life is one of joy. People will be drawn to us and to Him when they see the quality of joy that we experience. Even in painful circumstances which cause us to be emotionally unhappy, Christians can experience spiritual joy. Don't freeze up spiritually with analysis-paralysis. I'll say it once more for emphasis: We can just live, allowing Christ to naturally and normally express Himself through us.

On the night I lay on the floor crying in desperation, I felt that there was no real way to enjoy my faith in the way the Bible describes. Maybe you picked up this book feeling that way. The truths I have written about are not *theoretical* ideas which might bring joy to your Christian life. These are *actual* truths which have been tested and proven in my own life. Joy isn't an emotion, but a Person named Jesus. If a recovering "works-a-holic" like me can enter into a grace walk, you can too. It simply requires appropriating by faith that Christ is your life and then allowing Him to live His Life through you. I assume that because you have read this book you must have a hunger to experience His life to the fullest. Christ's life is experienced daily in the same way it was received initially—by faith.

I asked the Lord that night, "What do You want from me?" What does He want from us? He just wants *us*. Not our promises. Not our good intentions. Not even our Christian service. Everything else takes care of itself when we just rest in His arms, allowing Him to act through us. What a joy and a relief. It isn't a passive lifestyle, but a peaceful one where we actively rest in Him and He does it all. It is a walk of grace—and it really is amazing!

Chapter One

1. Charles G. Trumbull, *Victory in Christ* (Fort Washington, PA: Christian Literature Crusade, 1969), 18-19.

2. *Webster's Ninth Collegiate Dictionary* (Springfield, MA: Merriam-Webster, Inc., 1983), 678.

Chapter Two

1. Watchman Nee, *The Release of the Spirit* (Indianapolis: Sure Foundation Publishers, 1965), 10-11.

2. Peter Lord is pastor of Park Avenue Baptist Church in Titusville, Florida. He is also an author and travels extensively as a speaker in churches and conferences across America.

Chapter Three

1. Neil T. Anderson, *Victory Over the Darkness* (Ventura, CA: Regal Books, 1990), 43-44.

2. Bob George, *Classic Christianity* (Eugene, OR: Harvest House, 1989), 77-78.

3. *Ibid.*

Chapter Four

1. *Webster's Ninth Collegiate Dictionary* (Springfield, MA: Merriam-Webster, Inc., 1983), 667.

2. Bill Gillham, *Lifetime Guarantee* (Eugene, OR: Harvest House, 1987), 90.

3.   D. Martyn Lloyd-Jones, *Romans: The New Man* (Grand Rapids: Zondervan, 1972), 65.

4.   Charles Stanley, "The Sufficiency of Christ," a message preached at the First Baptist Church of Atlanta.

5.   Bill Gillham, *Lifetime Guarantee*, 90.

Chapter Five

1.   Grace Ministries International is an organization whose focus is to help the members of the body of Christ to experience, mature in, and effectively communicate the message of the cross, in all its implications, in their various spheres of influence, so that all may know Christ as Savior, Lord, and Life.

2.   In *Lifetime Guarantee*, Bill Gillham provides a thorough study of how the flesh develops in every person and how one may come to experience the abundant life that stems from appropriating Christ as life. It is a definitive work on this subject.

3.   These questions are not intended to suggest that the Christian life can be free of painful circumstances. The point to be understood is that while religious ritual is a tiring duty, when the Spirit of Christ ministers through us, the Christian life is a blessing and not a burden.

Chapter Six

1.   Watchman Nee, *The Normal Christian Life* (Wheaton, IL: Tyndale House, 1956), 155-156.

2.   DeVerne F. Fromke, *The Ultimate Intention* (Indianapolis: Sure Foundation, 1963), 83-84.

Chapter Seven

1. Major Ian Thomas, *The Saving Life of Christ* (Grand Rapids: Zondervan, 1961), 85.

2. Major Ian Thomas, *The Mystery of Godliness* (Grand Rapids: Zondervan, 1964), 258-259.

3. Charles G. Trumbull, *Victory in Christ* (Fort Washington, PA: Christian Literature Crusade, 1969), 47-49.

Chapter Eight

1. Vance Havner, *Pleasant Paths* (Grand Rapids: Baker Book House, 1983), 36.

Chapter Ten

1. Jack Taylor, *The Word of God with Power* (Nashville: Broadman & Holman Publishers, 1993), 17-18.

Chapter Eleven

1. DeVerne F. Fromke, *The Ultimate Intention* (Indianapolis: Sure Foundation, 1963), 55-56.

2. *Ibid.* 72-73. Quoting Watchman Nee.

3. Watchman Nee, *What Shall This Man Do?* (Fort Washington, PA: Christian Literature Crusade, 1961), 100.

Chapter Twelve

1. *Plato's The Republic* (Lincoln, NE: Cliff's Notes, Inc., 1963), 52-53.

2. *Ibid.* 33.

3. Andrew Murray, *Waiting on God* (Chicago: Moody Press, 1978), 60.

BIBLIOGRAPHY

Anderson, Neil. *Victory Over the Darkness.* Regal Books, 1990.

Cliff's Notes. *Plato's The Republic.* Cliff's Notes, Inc., 1963.

Fromke, DeVern F. *The Ultimate Intention.* Sure Foundation, 1963.

George, Bob. *Classic Christianity.* Harvest House Publishers, 1989.

George, Bob. *Growing in Grace.* Harvest House Publishers, 1991.

Gillham, Bill. *Lifetime Guarantee.* Harvest House Publishers, 1987.

Lloyd-Jones, D. Martyn. *Romans, The New Man* Zondervan Publishing House, 1973.

Murray, Andrew. *Waiting on God.* Moody Press, 1978

Nee, Watchman. *The Normal Christian Life.* Tyndale House Publishers, 1977.

Nee, Watchman. *The Release of the Spirit.* Sure Foundation, 1965.

Nee, Watchman. *What Shall This Man Do?* Christian Literature Crusade, 1961.

Taylor, Jack. *The Word of God with Power.* Broadman & Holman Publishers, 1993.

Thomas, Ian. *The Saving Life of Christ*. Zondervan
Publishing House, 1961.

Thomas, Ian. *The Mystery of Godliness*. Zondervan
Publishing House, 1964.

Trumbull, Charles. *Victory in Christ*. Christian Literature
Crusade, 1959.

STUDY GUIDE

Chapter 1 - Miserable Mediocrity

1. Describe the biblical meaning of success in the Christian life. Do you believe that most Christians have a proper understanding of success in life? Why or why not?

2. Can you relate to the motivation-condemnation-rededication cycle? What problems come from rededicating yourself to God and trying harder to live for Him? Discuss the difference between trying and trusting for victory in the Christian life.

3. Read Galatians 3:19-25. What is the purpose of the law? Describe the Christian who is living under the law instead of grace.

4. How has the focus on production and performance affected the modern church? How did the church of the New Testament differ in this regard?

5. Should Christians seek to find fulfillment in life from the things they do for God? Do you believe that most Christians are experiencing a sense of fulfillment in their lifestyle? Why or why not?

Chapter 2 - Darkness Before Dawn

1. Read Romans 12:1-2. Define your understanding of absolute surrender to God. What are the evidences that a person has absolutely surrendered himself to God?

2. *Flesh* refers to the learned strategies one utilizes to get his own needs met apart from Christ. Is walking after the flesh always repulsive? Describe Paul's flesh patterns as described in Philippians 3:3-7.

3.   Describe how a person's ability can become a liability to him spiritually. How might Christians unintentionally affirm and strengthen the flesh of other Christians?

4.   Steve suggests that trying to do something for God may sound admirable, but it produces damaging consequences. Do you agree or disagree? Why? Will God bless self-effort?

5.   Read Genesis 16:1-6. How did Abraham and Sarah try to help God? What were the consequences? Describe some ways that people may try to help God today. What is wrong with trying to help Him?

6.   How do you define brokenness? Steve asserts that God *will* put heavier burdens on us that we can bear. Do you agree? Why or why not?

7.   What is God's purpose in bringing a person to brokenness? Why would a loving God allow His children to experience pain?

8.   Luke 10:40-42 indicates that Martha was distracted from Jesus by serving Him. How might this be a danger in the lives of Christians today?

Chapter 3 - A Brand New Me

1.   What causes a Christian to be accepted by God? Does God totally accept us when our lifestyle is a contradiction of our profession? Explain your answer.

2.   Why is it important to understand our new identity in Christ? What is wrong with a person believing he is nothing more than a sinner saved by grace?

3.   Why do you suppose most unbelievers see themselves as pretty good people, yet many Christians see themselves as

nothing more than saved sinners? What is a saint?

4. Read Romans 9:30-10:4. The Jews tried to become righteous, yet failed, while the Gentiles did not try to become righteous, yet they attained it. Explain how this happened.

5. Explain why forgiveness alone is not enough to cause a person to experience victory in the Christian life.

6. Was Lot a godly man? Was his behavior godly? What is needed for a person to be rightfully called righteous?

Chapter 4 - A Dead Old Man

1. Read 2 Peter 1:4 and explain what way Christians become a partaker of the divine nature. Does a Christian have one or two natures?

2. Paul says in Galatians 2:20 that he had been crucified with Christ. In what sense are we crucified with Him? What power does sin have over believers today?

3. Comment on this statement: "The source of our old life has been cut away from us forever by the circumcision performed on us by the Spirit of God. When a Christian sins, he is acting in a way that is unnatural for him." Why does it sometimes seem so easy to sin?

4. If a Christian's sin nature is dead, is it possible to live without sin in this life? What causes a Christian to sin?

Chapter 5 - Experiencing His Life

1. How would you define "the exchanged life"? How does one experience this life? How does experiencing the exchanged life differ from a "second work of grace"?

2.   Do you believe the Christian life is hard or easy? What things might cause the Christian life to seem hard to live?

3.   What is the difference between religious activity at church and in spiritual service? Which characterizes your church?

4.   Read Matthew 11:28-30. Are most Christians experiencing what Jesus promised in these verses? Why or why not?

5.   Steve lists four reasons why believers may try to live the Christian life out of self-effort. Discuss these four. What other reasons could be listed?

6.   What does a Christian who is struggling to live for God need to understand? How do we reconcile the rest that Jesus described with the struggle Paul talked about in Ephesians 6:12?

Chapter 6 - Free from the Law

1.   What is a Christian legalist? How does legalism manifest itself in a person's lifestyle?

2.   Read 1 Corinthians 15:56 and Romans 7:5-6. What effect does living under law have on the Christian? Should a believer try to obey God's laws?

3.   What kinds of rules have you embraced as laws for your Christian life? According to Romans 7:1-4, what relationship does the believer have to the law?

4.   Does being free from the law mean that how we live is unimportant? What will ensure godly behavior if a Christian doesn't try to obey God's laws?

5.   Discuss this statement: "The core of the Christian life

doesn't revolve around doing, but is grounded in being."

6.   Steve suggests that the key to experiencing victory is not in rededicating yourself to God. Do you agree? Explain your answer.

Chapter 7 - Victory Is a Gift

1.   Discuss this statement: "Trying to do something for God is a flesh trip. It is possible to be sincere in trying to do something for Him, yet be sincerely wrong."

2.   What is wrong with centering our Christian life around serving God? Does God want us to serve Him?

3.   Explain the difference between the belief that Christ gives us victory and that He *is* our victory.

4.   Read Romans 8:5-6. How does this verse relate to overcoming sins that enslave a believer?

5.   Read Romans 5:10. Christians are saved from sin's penalty by Christ's death. How are we saved from its power by His life?

Chapter 8 - The Vice of Values

1.   Steve suggests that a Christian's life shouldn't be built around Christian values, but on the person of Christ. What is the difference between the two?

2.   Discuss this statement: "Before I understood that Christ is my life, my whole lifestyle was characterized by an obsession with right and wrong. Yet, if one is not abiding in Christ, every action is wrong."

3.   What place does the law of God have in contemporary society? Should Christians stress the law of God to unbelievers? Why or why not?

4. "Without the law a person has no gauge for right and wrong. The principle of right and wrong is inseparably linked to God's laws. They cannot be separated." How can this statement be reconciled with the fact that believers are dead to the law?

5. Describe the differences between being married to Mr. Law and Mr. Grace.

6. Read 1 Timothy 1:8-11. To what people has God given the law? Are all Christians righteous? What laws does God expect believers to embrace today?

Chapter 9 - All You Need Is Love

1. Read Luke 15:11-24. How did the prodigal son's failure to understand his identity interfere with the way he related to his father? How do you see yourself in this story?

2. Do you believe that it is important for a Christian to ask for forgiveness when he sins? Discuss the difference between confession of sin and asking for forgiveness. Do the sins of a Christian remain unforgiven if he doesn't ask God for forgiveness?

3. Read Romans 6:1-6. If God's grace has covered all of our sins, why don't Christians decide to enjoy themselves through a lifestyle of sin? What keeps you from choosing to sin when you resist temptation?

4. Discuss the difference between a law-oriented perspective and a grace-oriented view on the commandments of the New Testament.

5. What causes one's love for God to increase? Name some specific factors in your own life that have caused you to have a greater love for Him.

Chapter 10 - From Duty to Delight

1. Discuss this statement: "It was only after I began to understand grace that I realized that God never intended that we should live by the Bible." Why would it be a mistake to try to live by the Bible?

2. What is God's purpose in giving us the Bible?

3. Read 1 Thessalonians 5:17. How is it possible to pray without ceasing? How do you define a strong prayer life?

4. Discuss some of the specific times that God has spoken to you. Do you believe that God wants to speak to every Christian personally? How often?

5. Steve suggests that if we are abiding in Christ, it is impossible to get out of the will of God. Do you agree or disagree? Explain your answer.

6. How can a believer know the will of God?

7. In 1 Corinthians 2:16, Paul says, "But we have the mind of Christ." What does this mean? Does every Christian have the mind of Christ?

Chapter 11 - People Who Need People

1. Describe the different approaches taken in evangelism between a legalist and a person walking in grace. Which approach characterizes your own life? Why?

2. How might evangelism take on a workday approach? Is there a difference between sharing the "plan of salvation" and "sharing Christ"? Explain.

3. Discuss the differences between grace and mercy.

4. In what way is evangelism deficient if it emphasizes

receiving forgiveness without emphasizing the new life received at salvation? What will be the resulting consequences in the life of the new Christian?

5. How do you define the church? Name some specific ways that your church demonstrates the grace of God toward the world.

6. God's church is a diverse family. Is there a proper place for denominational distinctions? Read 1 Corinthians 12:12-13. In what ways are different churches interdependent on each other?

Chapter 12 - Living in Grace

1. In what ways do you see yourself in "The Allegory of the Cave"? What chains hold Christians in the cave of legalism?

2. Discuss the difference between biblical education and divine revelation. What are the dangers of education without revelation? How does a Christian experience divine revelation from God?

3. Read John 15:1-5. What does it mean to abide in Christ? How does a Christian abide in Him?

4. What is the difference between "the Christian religion" and biblical Christianity? Is "the Christian religion" better than other religions? Why or why not?

5. Discuss this statement: "When we are living each day abiding in Christ, we can do whatever we want to do."

6. What does God want from you?